STEALING
GYPSY TREASURE

STEALING GYPSY TREASURE

"America's Love Affair with the Gypsy and His Horse"

Joyce M. Christian

STEALING GYPSY TREASURE
"AMERICA'S LOVE AFFAIR WITH THE GYPSY AND HIS HORSE"

iUniverse books may be ordered through booksellers or by contacting:

iUniverse
1663 Liberty Drive
Bloomington, IN 47403
www.iuniverse.com
1-800-Authors (1-800-288-4677)

ISBN: 978-1-5320-5240-8 (sc)
ISBN: 978-1-5320-5239-2 (e)

Library of Congress Control Number: 2018906987

Print information available on the last page.

iUniverse rev. date: 07/18/2018

The author with yearling filly, "Shaylee's Bevin", followed by Dorothy Cleary with Golden Heart Vanners yearling filly, "Pot of Gold" aka "Twink". Photo courtesy Mark J. Barrett.

"The love of a horse is just as complicated as the love for another human being, if you never love a horse you will never understand. – Author Unknown

A DEDICATION

This book is for my grandchildren, Aidan, Emma, Sophie, and Ella. It is my hope that it will help them understand my personal passion and thereby begin to find and follow their own. The work is also dedicated to my daughter, Jill, whose interest in horseback riding made it possible for me to begin this journey.

I cannot in good conscience write any work about Gypsy Vanner Horses without also dedicating it to Cindy Thompson who saw a little black and white stallion running in a field and had the interest to pursue who he was. Also to her husband, Dennis, who long after Cindy was gone, has continued to build and preserve their dream; a dream that has given meaning and perspective to my own.

DISCLAIMER

The Gypsy Vanner Horse Society (GVHS) is and always will be my chosen registry for horses bred by Gypsies. As a member of this organization from its earliest beginnings, I have dedicated two decades of work towards its continued success. However, as with any and all horse registries, it too is a democratic organization and politics does play a role in its workings. Therefore, while it is my hope that this organization remains true to many of the foundational efforts described in this work, in reality I know the political structure can and may in time change its course. I have done my best to stay clear of actual registry business; any reference in this work to the GVHS is by means of historical reference and is in no way intended to be the current stance of the organization.

This work is therefore the result of independent research and personal experience. It should never be misunderstood as a work for the GVHS, but rather an independent undertaking by the author on behalf of the horses, given the name Gypsy Vanner Horse by Dennis and Cindy Thompson and Fred Walker. It is an attempt to record history; to view the horses identified in the Thompson study through the lens of breed development research; to pay respect to the foundational efforts of the Gypsy families whose herds became the standard when the Thompsons decided to declare them a breed; all through the eyes of a trained researcher whose personal journey with these horses began in 1995.

AN INTRODUCTION

It has been twenty plus years since the back door of an arena in Germany opened and I set eyes for the first time on an incredibly unique horse. At the time, I had no idea what the horse was, where it came from, and why it was in the modern world of the 1990's I had not seen this remarkable equine before.

It was the mid 90's. The horse was brown and white; had a mane and tail a fairytale horse would envy and feathered feet that added to its ethereal beauty. When I asked my daughter's riding instructor what breed of horse this was and where did it come from, he simply replied, "It is a horse from the Gypsies."

I was curious to say the least. Being an educator and therefore trained observer, I began to attempt to find answers to even the simplest questions:

- Is this a breed or a crossbred animal?
- Who are the Gypsies responsible for breeding this horse?
- Why have we not seen these horses until now?
- Why is there such a variable difference in quality and appearance in colored horses coming from Gypsies?

For two years, I would observe, question and try and find some understanding of how this horse had come to be. Then one night in 1998 I was sitting at my home computer and I typed in the search box, "horses from Gypsies", and a website with a beautiful black and white horse rearing in a crystal ball appeared. It was the website of Dennis and Cindy Thompsons' farm, Gypsy Gold. As I read their story of how they had found the horses and then began a search to understand them I was overcome with excitement. I had found a wonderful source to begin to answer my many questions.

While the Thompsons' work is the cornerstone, my search to understand these horses has been ongoing for the last twenty plus years now. It has been a love affair and at the same time: a study of the horses, of the people behind the horse, of the Americans who embraced the horse, and the ongoing conflicts and politics that undoubtedly appear when introducing and preserving a breed for the future.

An introduction to the name......

Why Gypsy Vanner Horse? Why not Gypsy Cob, Gypsy Horse, or Gypsy?

We can all recall that day in English Literature class when we first heard that ever famous Shakespearean quote:

"What's in a name? That which we call a rose by any other name would smell as sweet."- Juliet

- Romeo and Juliet (II, ii, 1-2)

No matter how Romeo Montague and Juliet Capulet wanted it to be otherwise, their names would have a meaning they could not escape. While Juliet ponders the idea that a rose would smell just as sweet if called by another name – she is most certainly correct; yet she was who she was; her family name held meaning, set her apart, and would determine her destiny.

Close your eyes and say rose – four simple letters. Yet when heard, when spoken, when even thought about all of our senses bring to mind the color, the smell, the shape, the thorns, the romance, the beauty that is the flower known by its name, rose.

In the horse world names also carry meaning. They cause us to see and understand the characteristics that establish and signify each breed.

When we hear Thoroughbred, we see the horse, we think of Churchill Downs on a weekend in May, big hats, a bell, a victory, and a blanket of roses. When we hear Clydesdale, we know the horse, we think of beer, a wagon, a team of eight, power, beauty, and commercials that make us laugh and cry.

In the world of horses bred by Gypsies it has been, or so it seems, an ongoing battle of the names. Why? The truth, well, most are confused by all the names; some would like to skip over the name thing; but just as in Juliet's case there is a name, carefully chosen, put in place at the time of breed recognition, with meaning and purpose, that name is Gypsy Vanner Horse.

In 1994 there was no name for the horse that would earn the name Gypsy Vanner. There were about four thousand horses bred by the Gypsies of the United Kingdom that were known simply as colored cobs, or colored horses. For hundreds of years Gypsies had bred horses; gone about their daily lives enjoying and using their horses for varied work, while the outside world showed no interest. But something happened between 1950 and 1990 that changed all that.

Lifestyle changes, government regulation, and economy would change the way Gypsies bred horses. They bred for broken coats and without the need for larger living wagons; they naturally bred for a smaller, more economical horse. Around 1950 they were simply focused on coat color and average size. With those two things in mind most Gypsies continued to breed as they had always done – indiscriminately – breeding what you have to what you can find; now with broken coat and smaller being their only requirements.

However, a few Gypsy men, among them Fred Walker, Patsy McCann, Robert Watson, John Pratt, Tom Price, Sydney Harker, and a handful more decided to breed differently. As these men looked at the bow top caravans, now the wagon of choice, they saw the color and magic of their culture showcased in these brightly decorated wagons. The art work was captivating and celebrated a bit of whom and what they were as a people. They began to envision a horse as colorful and fanciful as the wagon it would pull. For the first time in history a group of Gypsies decided to breed selectively.

Twenty years into the process and the British and Irish folk still did not see what was happening right in their own backyards. Why? In their minds, Gypsies don't have any horses of value; they breed what they have to what they can find.

At the same time within the Gypsy community the herds from these men were becoming highly sought after and prized. Many of these breeders began hiding their choice stallions and mares for fear they would be stolen – by other Gypsies; or, even worse, killed to prevent establishing the line. In the late 1990's and even after I returned home to the USA in 2001 I came across such stories. Horses hidden deep in wooded areas, under bridges, or left with local farmers to guard.

Robert Watson was known for hiding his prized stallion, Lad – aka Watson's Old Horse/Tom, a direct son of The Roadsweeper UK and grandson of The Coal Horse. This stallion had once been poisoned and due to his value Watson began hiding him for his safety.

By the 1990's these selectively bred herds began to stand out from their distant cousins, the many indiscriminately bred colored cobs making up the bulk of the UK's colored horse population. While the British, Irish and even the Gypsies themselves began to see something special in certain herds, they still showed no interest in understanding or explaining this difference. They began on the other hand to simply label them, "good ones" or "now that's a proper cob"; nothing more, nothing less.

Neighboring German horse enthusiasts began to show an interest, but even they could not bring themselves to distinguish a division in the colored cob population. However, these people know horses and recognize that all need a name. So, they added the label, Tinker Horse, to the now growing list of labels for these colored horses from the Gypsies. Yet, like all the others this label also stood for any and all colored horses being bred by Gypsies.

In 1994 GVHS Co-Founders, Dennis and Cindy Thompson, would first see Cushti Bok and for most of you reading this you know the story or if not you can read it on the Gypsy Gold website at *www.gypsygold. com*. That moment in time was the turning point for recognizing a breed.

What is a breed? While breed development specialists, Dr. Phillip Sponenberg and Dr. Donald Bixby, explain the term can be interpreted both loosely and restrictively, most horse enthusiasts use the more restrictive version when establishing a group of horses as a distinctive group of animals capable of consistently reproducing themselves.

Believing there was a genetic base behind the favored phenotype, the Thompsons set out to answer their question; was Cushti Bok a purebred animal or was he nothing more than a lucky cross? Sound familiar, yes, these were the same questions I too had begun to ask as I stood in a German riding arena and wondered about a horse unlike any I had ever seen before.

When the Thompsons imported the first of these horses and established the first registry to begin to track phenotype and bloodlines of the best they had found, it was indeed a first. While Gypsies had been breeding horses for generations, their work to create these horses had been done so quietly even the Irish and British equestrian communities had overlooked the development of a breed worthy group.

The Gypsy men behind the selective herds took great pride in their horses. In the 1990's you could if you studied the herds see the personal stamp of each of these breeders on their herds. At the same time, you could see the shared quality that the selective breeding process had brought to this special group. These breeders welcomed the Thompsons into their world not as buyers, but as people who saw in their special horses what they themselves valued.

As the Thompsons traced Cushti Bok's lineage they began to see the connections between breeders and the selection of sires and dams that had created this truly unique group of colored horses. My desire to understand caused me to track the horses coming and going through our local riding stable in Germany. I also watched with curiosity the importing of horses once I returned to the USA. I began to understand that maybe even without meaning to do so, the Gypsy culture had through their love of the horse, and a lifestyle that was disappearing, created a new breed, not yet recognized even in its country of origin.

"In 2005 my mare, Magic, gave birth to a colt by Cushti Bok. His name is "Cushti Bok's Lord Marlborough, aka, Lordi". This was a dream come true on so many levels. Today, that colt is a wonderful stallion, who greets me every morning, with a whinny to remind me of exactly who he is and why that is important." This wonderful photo is courtesy of our friend, Mark J. Barrett.

Now, what to do?

The Thompsons took the first steps. They sat with mentor and friend, Fred Walker, and talked about the pros and cons of this adventure they were about to embark upon. Nothing about it would be easy; because everything about it was complex – the population of colored horses, the Gypsy culture, and the economic principle of supply and demand. But Gypsy breeders were already breeding away from "this Cushti Bok like horse". They were breeding for even smaller horses and ponies. If the Thompsons ignored this and let it go, the horses they had just seen, and had come to understand might possibly be lost, with most of the world never being able to see and appreciate what these few Gypsy breeders had accomplished.

If they went forward they risked having the Gypsy community bombarded by eager buyers anxious to buy, breed, and sell horses. Was this fair to a culture known for its privacy, secrecy, and preference to be apart from even the cultures with which it shared a country?

Knowing at the time that the selective herds they had come to understand comprised only approximately twenty percent of the total Gypsy colored cob population, there simply would not be enough of these horses to meet the demand they would create.

For the Thompsons, it had become unthinkable to not at least make the effort to honor these men and their truly treasured accomplishment. Therefore, only going forward with the approval of their mentor, Fred Walker, aka *King of the Coloured Horses*, a title bestowed on him by his peers. Together, they began to search for and agree on a name – not for any and all colored cobs, but for the prized herds, the twenty percent; the selectively bred herds of those few men, the horses whose pedigrees had been traced back to two founding stallions, The Coal Horse, and Sonny Mays. Whose phenotypes grounded in those genetics exhibited characteristics that clearly set them apart from the common cob, and trade horse populations.

After a time of discussion and deliberation they would choose the name, Gypsy Vanner Horse. Gypsy – to honor the men, who had selectively bred herds the Thompsons had uncovered, Vanner – for the job of pulling the bow top caravans, and Horse – for the species.

With the name, Gypsy Vanner Horse, for the first time in history a group of horses bred by Gypsies was identified as a definitive, phenotypically understood, genetic based breed and that breed now had a name.

The Gypsy culture's inclination for horse trading kicked into gear when the Thompsons introduced the newly recognized and named breed, the Gypsy Vanner Horse. Unfortunately, without a careful study into Gypsy breeding practices, the many American first-time encounters with Gypsies and their horses could and would result in the buying, selling, and trading of all colored cobs and trade horses.

The breed name, Gypsy Vanner Horse, and its registry, the Gypsy Vanner Horse Society, were not originally established for the whole of the population, therefore industry politics came into play and old labels re-surfaced as if they were names for a breed – Gypsy Cob, Gypsy Horse, and even just Gypsy.

First establishing and then honoring a new breed is never easy; its path to preservation more often than not is paved by all these age-old breed development problems. The Gypsy Vanner Horse is no exception.

The introduction you have just read is really a brief synopsis of the events leading up to the study and understanding of a group of horses bred by Gypsies, recognized as breed worthy, and then named, Gypsy Vanner Horse. For me it has been an incredible, more often than not difficult journey. It will be necessary to break down the parts of the story and go into more detail in order to shed light on a better understanding of this horse. As with most authors who set out to find and then share truth those endeavors are often plagued with obstacles and it is not always easy to find absolutes. The horse industry for the most part is about horse trading – the buying and selling of horses. While most people who would eventually be drawn to this horse would do so from that perspective, mine was solely a quest for knowledge, then a professional need to teach and share what I had learned. With that as a foundation I invite you to join me on this most fascinating quest I undertook now some twenty years ago. I begin with a Gypsy proverb I uncovered in my research:

"He who is about to tell the truth should have one foot in the stirrup."

CHAPTER
One

The People Behind the
Horse – A Brief History

In the mid 1990's if someone mentioned Gypsy I immediately thought of a beautiful dark haired girl in colorful flowing skirts and scarves with a mysterious aura about her. Never had I thought about a culture that would because of who they are; create an incredible new breed of horse I would come to love.

Yet when I first asked about these unusual animals I was told they were from the Gypsies. It was time to get to know these people behind this horse. Initially I found very few books with historical information. Most were biographies with a focus on a particular person rather than Gypsies as a group.

It wasn't until a few years ago that a friend gave me a book entitled, *"A History of The Romani People"* by Hristo Kyuchukov and Ian Hancock that my understanding into these remarkable people began to grow. The book was a children's picture book with just enough information to whet my appetite. I then discovered that Dr. Hancock had written a history of the Romani, *"We Are the Romani"*, and I checked it out of the library and delved into the thousand years of these people's travels and troubles.

A thousand years ago a Muslim group invaded India and took captive a caste of people called the *Rajput*. Many of this group were enslaved, injured, or killed. Some eventually would escape and move on. A group ended up in the Kingdom of Rum which would become modern day Turkey. It is from this group the name *Romani* is said to have originated. These people eventually found their way to the British Iles in the late 1400's and early 1500's. The people came with their belongings. According to British equestrian and author, Edward Hart, they came in bender tents and with their donkeys.

In addition to the Romani we also find the Irish Travellers, a group also falling under the umbrella word of "Gypsy". While both groups have similar interest in the traveling lifestyle, they also hold clear differences that set them apart from each other. While the Romani take great pride in their history, the Travellers have yet an ongoing debated origin.

It is not my purpose in this work to delve into these differences but to rather embrace all Gypsy connected groups within the United Kingdom whose lifestyle of traveling resulted in a special love for horses. It was this lifestyle, this connection with horses, and their shared appreciation for natural beauty that caused these amazing people to create a new horse.

Wanderlust appeared to be innate to these people; they preferred to be on the go rather than settled. This came from an admiration and genuine love of the natural world. It also was further inspired by their ongoing search for adventure. Each day was a gift, simply waiting to be unwrapped by setting out on the open road in search of what lay ahead. In *"Stopping Places"* by Simon Evans we find this wonderful quote from Gypsy, Ambrose Cooper:

"The only thing a Gypsy had was a sense of freedom, you had nothing to tie you down, you could go where you liked and travel where you liked. When God made Earth, He made it for man to walk in, to be free. Not for someone to own and stop someone else from walking around it, which is what's happened today. That's the way the Gypsy looks at the world as somewhere for a man to walk, not for someone to put a gate up and put "Private" on it and say, "You can't walk on this land because I own it." (Evans 1999, ii)

For the Gypsy culture, the world belongs to us all; it is to be shared; to be enjoyed; to be experienced in special ways day by day. No such thing as long term planning; putting down roots. Those ideas and way of life put unnecessary limits on the Gypsy's free spirit.

This delightful poem by Michael J. Chalcraft from *"Gypsy Memories"* by Barrie Law, provides a window for us to get a glimpse of this somewhat carefree life on the open road *(Law 2000, 3)*:

A Fortunate Call

After travelling all day through the wind and the rain,
We stopped for the night down a muddy old lane.
We then lit a fire and had something to eat.
After a day on the road, it went down a treat.
The next day I went hawking to try'n make some dosh,
And I called at a house that looked rather posh.
"Would you buy a few pegs or a nice piece of lace?"
"Come in", said the lady with a smile on her face.
She bought some lace and a dozen pegs too.
And then she asked, "Is it really true?"
"Is it true that the Gypsies will bring you good luck?"
After paying me well, which I gratefully took,
"Good luck", I said, "Is in the lap of the gods,
But we'll do what we can to shorten the odds."

The poem clearly tells us about possible Gypsy jobs. The occupations found most often within the Gypsy culture were those that would be appropriate for people on the move. They were skilled laborers, artisans, and entertainers. One of their most prized skills was that of horsemanship. According to Dr. Kyuchukov and Dr. Hancock, *"....these people have been buying, selling, and trading horses as a profitable profession for hundreds of years." (A History of The Romani People, Kyuchukov/Hancock 2005, 11)*

Eventually they would trade their tents for living wagons. Basically, these were the first mobile homes, a house on wheels. They traveled in large groups throughout the countryside, stopping for work in the villages; when found setting up their camps just outside the town. Their chief form of transportation was the horse. In fact, Gypsies and their horses were inseparable as this old saying indicates, *"A Gypsy without a horse is no Gypsy."*

At the turn of the last century, the early 1900's their horse of choice was a large draft type animal. This was a horse strong and calm enough to perform the much-needed task of pulling the family's living wagon from place to place. When at rest, these horses were tended by the family and frequently by the children. They had to be of a quiet and manageable temperament. Because they were so crucial to the family's wellbeing they were viewed as family.

Originally Gypsies were poor and could afford only such horses as other people would not want. In the early 1900's these were their horses. They kept horses they called family and horses they traded or sold as a means of livelihood. To build their herds they had but one breeding plan, breed what you have to what you can find. One of the things they would do that often angered the townspeople or local farmers was to put a mare in heat overnight in a field where a farmer's stallion was kept. Should the mare be in foal as a result of this tryst then so be it and the better for it. Most often the Gypsy would move on and the farmer would not even know what had transpired.

Rachel Morris and Luke Clements provide insight into changes that brought about shifts in the Gypsy preferred way of life in their edited version of, *"Gaining Ground: Law Reform for Gypsies and Travellers"*:

"In the years before WWI Gypsies and Travellers enjoyed a relatively undisturbed existence, which changed little despite the introduction of planning regulation. After WWII the picture began to change; first with highway and motorway construction taking away traditional stopping places on green verges and the like; then the Commons Registration Act 1960 comprehensively changed the availability of common land for winter stopping. The Act placed ownership of the Commons into Local Authority or "commoners' hands". For the first time, trespass laws could be enforced against those stopping on the Commons. At the same time the changes to a more modern mechanic-based agriculture industry meant the end of farmers' need to accommodate seasonal labor in the spring and summer months." (Morris/Clements 1999)

The World Wars came. The British government confiscated horses from the Gypsies for wartime use. Why? They had the perfect horses; large draft crosses capable of pulling heavy loads over long distances while being calm and manageable. Following World War II the Gypsies returned to their travelling only to find British legislation being passed to limit their much-loved way of life. Laws were passed to prohibit travel in caravans. Eventually they shifted from their large living wagons to the smaller bow top caravans more suitable for short term travel and lodging. Many opted to keep their large living wagons, found a place to park it and lived in it for the rest of their lives. The younger ones travelled for fun and festivals rather than as a lifestyle and for them the bow top was perfect.

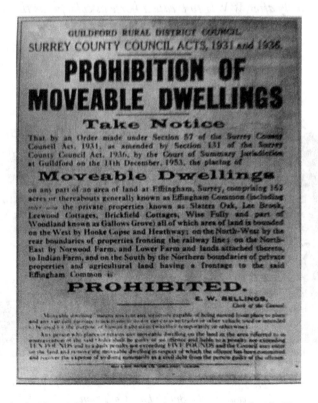

One of hundreds of posted notices to warn the Gypsies in England. (From the archives of Dr. Ian Hancock.)

With the enforced legislation in place and with the recent wartime confiscation of horses by the government the Gypsy horsemen began to envision a different horse. It would need to be a horse the government would not want; it would need to be a smaller horse more suitable to pull the bow top caravan; yet it would need to retain the desired traits they had so loved in their large draft crosses.

It would be these men with their desire to create the "perfect horse to pull their caravans", which would birth a new breed yet unachieved or ever before imagined. According to Edward Hart in *"The Coloured Horse and Pony"* he states, *"in the 1950's parti-coloureds rose in value and became status symbols to the travelling people." (Hart 1993, 63)* According to the foundational efforts of the Gypsy Vanner Horse Society, *"a vision was born shortly after WWII to create a horse as colorful as the caravan it would pull." (Thompson 1998)*

Fred Walker, aka "King of the Coloured Horses" sitting on the steps of his wagon. Photo courtesy the Barrie Law Collection.

CHAPTER
Two

The Gypsies and Their Horse
- My First Encounter

In 1995 my daughters and I had moved to Bitburg, Germany. I was a school administrator for the Department of Defense Schools and had received an assignment to Bitburg Elementary School. We found a wonderful house in the little village of Biersdorf and to my delight a riding stable was located about two blocks down the hill from our house.

I had loved horses all my life and wanted very much for my two daughters to also have that desire. Up until this time neither had shown any interest. However, one day my youngest, Jill, said she wanted to take riding lessons. I will always be grateful to her for that decision for without it I doubt I would have become involved with the Gypsy Vanner Horse.

Her riding instructor had begun to import horses from the British Gypsies for his riding program. What fascinated me most was the varied quality in the horses. While he maintained a group of what he called his show horses he also had about fifteen to twenty ordinary common cobs that he used in his day to day riding lessons and trail rides. All of these horses from Gypsies were "*coloured* horses", piebald (black and white) and skewbald (brown and white/or any other color and white) and a few tricolored horses usually black, brown and white. Occasionally there would be a solid with white feathers, but in the late 1990's this was very rare. They were all feathered horses and had more mane and tail than most I had come in contact with in my life.

His show horses were extraordinary. They were elegant in appearance; had an abundance of mane, tail, and feathering, and when at the trot possessed a movement unique to them. They learned quickly and seemed to have an uncanny willingness to please their young riders. For months, I observed these incredible animals always with an insatiable wonder as to how they had been bred. When I approached the riding instructor he would always tell me they were horses from Gypsies and these were some of the best. When I asked about speaking to the Gypsy with whom he was doing business he was reluctant to give out that information.

Finally, I stopped asking and continued to observe with a passion. I took long strolls through what he called his "Sale Barn" taking note of the similar traits I had come to recognize in the horses he called "the good ones". Unfortunately, these were extremely rare. It wasn't until I was able to purchase one of my own that I began to truly appreciate what these horses had to offer.

My first purchase was a three-year old, piebald filly. My daughter named her, Magic. When I asked my daughter's instructor about the Gypsy who had owned Magic, once again I encountered a reluctance to share anything at all about where the horse came from and who her breeder was. This continued to puzzle me. Why would the people behind this horse not be proud and pleased that others were now interested in them? Happy to have the horse I rather chose at that time to just enjoy her, and to let her teach me about who she was.

Our delightful mare, Magic. Photo courtesy Mark J. Barrett.

Time with this horse would just increase my questions. The level of intelligence was evident in ways that demonstrated intuitiveness, a gentle caution (an awareness not to hurt or harm), and a real desire to be close to these people she now found in her life. With each passing day, my love for this horse grew and so did my desire to better understand her and others like her.

Eventually I told, Rudy, my daughter's instructor, I wanted a second horse. Delighted with the thought of another sale he began to make suggestions. I told him I had found the horse, a solid black stallion with a white blaze and four white feathered feet in his sale barn. Just a few days earlier Rudy had found me peering into the horse's stall and had quickly told me the horse wasn't for sale. The horse had been sent for consideration to a lady in southern Germany, but now had returned and I decided to try once again.

It was clear; Rudy was somewhat concerned to contact the Gypsy owner. It had been explained the horse was in route back to England. Given the quality of the horse the Gypsy had decided he wanted the horse back, when his friend in southern Germany shared the three-year old stallion posed a risk on trails.

After much pleading Rudy finally agreed to call the Gypsy and let me speak with him. The man asked me why I was interested in his horse. It was only when he clearly understood the depth of my appreciation he decided "I had earned the horse". I not only described the desired traits the Gypsy culture had begun to admire, but I had also touched the "real reason" Gypsies have horses. Accepting that he did not wish to sell the animal, I told the man when his horse returned to England he would take my heart with him. At which point there was a long pause and then came the unexpected, "Well then, if he has your heart he does not belong to me any longer", said the proud Gypsy who had bred this wonderful horse. The beautiful black horse became mine. I named him Bandit.

Even with this personal connection, I was never allowed to know who the Gypsy was or where he lived. This simply was their way, make the sale, share the beauty of the horse, but keep the outsider at a proper distance, after all I was not family. This was my first encounter with a Gypsy. Why in the world would you not want people to know who you are and what you had in these amazing animals? A private culture, carefully guarding their secrets had developed over a thousand years of hardships. While they would have preferred to keep it so, the gold they had refined had begun to attract the outside world.

I loved having the horses in my life. I wanted to better understand them and to learn how the Gypsy culture had done this; unfortunately, I was working full time as a school administrator and trying to raise two teenage daughters on my own. There simply was no time to travel to England and do the required research to answer all my questions at that time. Rather, I let my two incredible horses begin to teach me about who they were.

My one and only Bandit, the horse who stole my heart. Photo courtesy Mark J. Barrett.

With the arrival of Bandit into my life, I now had two horses in my personal scope. The teacher in me simply was not satisfied with the lack of information and the secrecy that seemed to surround these horses from Gypsies. While the horses themselves, were fascinating and provided me with ongoing knowledge about their abilities and their unusual traits, I still wanted to know the people behind the horse.

In 1998 I found Dennis and Cindy Thompsons' website and felt I had stumbled upon an accurate source to begin to answer many of my questions. I encourage my readers to visit the Gypsy Gold website and read the Thompson story. I began communicating with the Thompsons via email in 1998. An appreciation for their work began and continues to this day.

CHAPTER
Three

Understanding A Landrace

So much of the last twenty years of my life has been spent defending the early work of Dennis and Cindy Thompson. I have told the story of how they found Cushti Bok so many times it is like second nature to me. My work and that of the Thompsons became entwined when I returned to the United States in 2001, because I, along with those early buyers of Gypsy Gold stock, could appreciate what their efforts meant. However, it wasn't long before I would learn that just like the horses we were small in number. Many people getting into these horses were not looking to the Thompsons as the standard, they were in this to make a mark for themselves. It would be years later as I began to study breed development research I would begin to get my mind around the politics that invade the horse industry, many times hampering the recognition and further development of breeds. Even when I began this book it was as if I felt the need to once again put on a defense and prepare for political battle. As I got further into this work I found myself reiterating the steps taken by the Thompsons to recognize these horses as a breed. While there are, and will be references to their work, I had to rethink this as I wanted to make certain people realize while the establishment of the registry by the Thompsons should in my humble opinion be understood as the founding event for a breed, it should not be the only source for understanding that breed.

The establishment of the world's first registry for any of the colored horses bred by Gypsies, the Gypsy Vanner Horse Society, has for me and I believe it should for the horse industry as well, remain a pivotal point. However, it certainly was not the beginning of my story with these horses. It certainly was not the beginning of these horses, because they were bred by Gypsies.

When I began my personal journey with two horses and a lot of questions, I really knew nothing about the horse industry and how it works. I was and probably still am to some extent naïve. I thought everyone cared about purity of breed. This is what had caused my questions. Was this horse I had come to admire a breed? And by that I meant genetic based not just a type of horse. If there was a group that had a genetic history and reproductive consistency, then why hadn't anyone already started some kind of organized record keeping for this group?

I love history and science. It was from this background that my interest grew. I truly sat out to understand a group of animals, at no time did I think about the financial benefits if any; whether I could get rich or lose everything; those of you who own horses know it can go either way. At the time, I had no idea how driven the horse industry is by horse trading. It really is all about buying, selling, and trading animals; not so much about the love of the horse. Yet, what history and science were revealing to me was that this horse, this "new breed", had been created for maybe no other reason at all, except "the love of the horse".

While breeds such as the Thoroughbred and Quarter Horse definitely developed from a performance perspective – racing horses, faster horses, horses that could go fast for a quarter mile. The Gypsy culture focused not on performance, rather it was all about keeping horses in their lives. Historically Gypsies have always had horses, early on it was because they needed them for transportation, but once the gasoline engine came on the scene most people put the horse aside. Those with horses began to refer to this activity as a hobby, no longer a necessity. The Gypsy on the other hand was carefully, and meticulously managing to maintain horses as a part of their lifestyle. The handling of horses was a highly regarded skill and proudly shared from father to son.

As I looked even more closely at this culture and this group of colored horses they had somehow generated, I came to understand the depth of family pride and the love of these animals involved. This was different; different on so many levels.

The problem was that nobody seemed to care.

The horse industry with its age-old engine, horse trading – the buying, selling, and trading of horses was swallowing this small group of animals whole, before anyone had the chance to see, question, and come to recognize the intricacies that if understood could and would set these horses apart from anything before or presently appreciated within the horse industry.

My work in the last decade has been focused on declaring this breed genetic based rather than type. From day one when I first saw a horse who could qualify as a Gypsy Vanner Horse it was about the genetic base for me. I knew enough to know that someone somewhere was carefully choosing their breeding stock, in order to end up with these remarkably beautiful and gifted horses. Gifted? Yes, they were consistently intelligent and willing. I know that we have intelligent and willing horses of all breeds, but I am talking percentages here. Along with their physical beauty, I saw consistency in these two other desirable traits as well. This was different and worth asking why.

I remember not too long ago while I was serving on the Board of Directors for the Gypsy Vanner Horse Society, my idea of genetic based rather than type was beginning to get on some folks' nerves. I wanted the Society to identify and embrace a genetic core, while welcoming horses with correct type to grow and build bloodlines. I felt then and I do now that this is the only way to preserve the horse of the 1990's that had earned the name, Gypsy Vanner Horse.

The big hurdle to overcome was how do you identify that core? I knew this was not going to be an easy task, but I still believed it was one that at least should be attempted. Why?

It all centers on breed development research and how the Gypsy culture from 1950 through the 1990's started from scratch and created one of the world's most undeniably beautiful equines. The first time I read the work of Dr. Phillip Sponenberg and Dr. Donald Bixby my excitement grew. In their work, *"Managing Breeds for a Secure Future"* they outline how to identify and preserve a group of animals as a definitive breed. They give us the necessary elements to study: history, phenotype, pedigree, performance and politics.

If you use this as your guide you find historically this group of colored horses which had developed seemingly from nowhere would meet the description of a landrace. Landrace breeds represent an early stage of breed development. They are sometimes referred to as "local breeds" or "natural breeds" due to isolation and selection environment setting the stage for people beginning to see them as breeds or certainly as animals with common traits. The group begins as crosses. This is exactly what happened with the Gypsy culture. In the 1950's they bred what they had to what they could find, yet at that time due to outside influences they began to focus on color pattern and smaller horses.

Initially horses being bred within the Gypsy culture throughout the United Kingdom were genetically variable and understood as crossbred. However, given time and looking at the cultural boundaries within which these breeders were operating we begin to see herds with broken coats and much smaller than the early draft crosses appearing towards the end of the 1950's. Particularly in Ireland the cob body type had become a favorite. In fact, the Gypsy Vanner Horse Society prides itself in saying that its roots lie with two Irish bred stallions, Sonny Mays and The Coal Horse.

By the 1970's this isolated group of colored horses, now with a recognized phenotype, that being the cob type began to attract attention. Remember we want to follow the progression of a genetic base. When a group of animals consistently reproduces a type, we can say they are growing more genetically uniform. However, if we stop there without taking this to the next level, research tells us that in time that much desired type can and more likely than not will be lost. Why? It is not difficult to capture type in crossbreeding. A good example of this is the Pinto. The Pinto is a recognized type breed. The only trait that is necessary for identification is the color pattern. The animal can be a pony, a horse; it can be tall, short; heavy or light and be a Pinto. Therefore, the Pinto is not a genetically uniform breed. If I breed two

Pintos I am not guaranteed the offspring will look like its parents; it could, or it could not.

As breeders become more selective with regards to traits things shift. By the 1990's some of the horses within the colored cob population being bred by Gypsies possessed a set of traits that began to set them apart from the other Gypsy bred animals. The color pattern was there, the type – cob body was there, but now there were even more recognizable traits. The appearance of more hair with the fuller mane and tail, and abundant feather on the feet were adding to the beauty of these horses. The draftiness in the heads was being eased out and these new horses' heads had an elegance and refinement in their appearance. Their conformation also gave way to movement exhibiting a trot soon becoming signature. The one performance element being retained by these ambitious breeders was the skill to pull. After all these horses were being bred to respect and honor tradition and a family's relationship with its horses.

By the time the Thompsons stumbled upon Cushti Bok, and I sat in a German riding arena and came face to face with a horse named Buck and then fell in love with a horse named, Bandit, it was clear the genetics in at least a portion of the landrace were solid. As the Thompsons traced Bok's lineage and met with many Gypsy men involved in the development of these horses it became clear it was a landrace with which they were dealing. There were breeders who were still crossbreeding and working on their own personal preferences. While at the same time a group of British Gypsies had through their careful breeding choices moved their herds further along the genetic continuum towards uniformity, consistency, the necessary strength to guarantee foals would be like their parents over and over again. It was this tiny portion of this landrace that had reached all the requirements to be classified as a standardized breed. It was this group that the original standard with its seven elements captured. It was this percentage that had been recognized for the first time as having the potential to have a future as a recognized breed. In 1996 this small percentage was given the name Gypsy Vanner Horse.

In the 1990's the number of these horses was extremely small in comparison to say a well- established breed such as the Arabian. Arabians exist in many countries all over the world; they are protected by a breed registry with a standard for their breeders to follow. We could say they have a sufficient number to maintain the group as a breed for years to come. Whereas, this tiny group of colored cob type horses being bred by Gypsies primarily in Ireland and England were just coming on the world scene. Culturally it was not important to the Gypsies for their horses to be anywhere outside of their community. They were not breeding these animals to compete on the world stage; while as a culture they are understood to be great horsemen, the purpose was so very different from that of breeders of other breeds. If we miss this, we miss the true fragile nature of this tiny group of animals that suddenly found itself in the spotlight, at a time in history when information could be shared in an instant resulting in an environment which made determining truth from lies quite difficult.

Establishing the Gypsy Vanner Horse Society as a private registry the Thompsons stated clearly in the beginning, their research had shown, only twenty percent of the colored cob population can qualify as Gypsy Vanner Horses. People didn't get this, they felt it was a marketing ploy, a get rich quick scheme set in motion by the Thompsons to sell their stock at high prices. Therefore, American buyers went to the United Kingdom, some for the right reasons, some for purely selfish ones, and they bought and brought back to America all the variety the landrace of colored cobs had to offer.

What does this mean? We are talking about numbers; we have to talk about numbers. Then we have to talk about how to breed to preserve a particular set of traits. That small group of British Gypsy breeders had discovered they had to be truly selective in their breeding choices to grow their herds with the look that had captured those of us who encountered these horses in the mid to late 1990's. The total colored cob population in the '90's was estimated to be around four to five thousand animals. From that group, which ones do we want to breed?

You want to find the ones whose genetic base is the strongest for reproducing the desired phenotype.

Within the landrace, it was clear a sufficient number of animals existed to reproduce color patterns and cob body type consistently. If we study the history, we understand why those two traits were carried throughout the population. Those two traits were obvious even in the one- time crosses, and had become solid for the bulk of the landrace. This we recognize as early breed development. Truly this population was becoming type driven. However, the question I asked and the one I believe the Thompsons found the answer to in their tracing of Bok's lineage was within this population is there a group that has reached a level of genetic strength which consistently puts the parents' quality in its foals, year after year?

The answer was yes, but the group was so small it was going to be difficult to first get people to understand not all the horses in this colored cob landrace were genetically strong; secondly, as a result there would be a need to help breeders specifically understand the whole of the population so as to protect rather than dilute the small genetic base that did exist in the late 1990's.

Were we successful in accomplishing that daunting task? Sadly, I am afraid we did not. Two decades after the spotlight fell on our little band of four to five thousand colored cobs, it is clear that rather than understanding the levels of genetic consistency or lack thereof within the population, America has just been breeding all over the population, sometimes growing the consistency, and at other times diluting it. As a result, now in 2018 the question is being asked over and over on the internet, in chat forums, why are we seeing such variety in these horses coming from the Gypsies?

When working within a landrace and knowingly utilizing type based animals, a careful breeder can over time through selection grow the genetic uniformity of herds eventually creating a standardized breed. When the Gypsy Vanner Horse Society was formed in 1996 as a private registry, the founders planned to do just that. Build a breed on the best-known bloodlines that were consistently producing the desired type, then given time and selection build the genetic base. Breed development research suggests that is a good plan, given the nature of the population of colored horses. However, I am willing to personally say I believe a genetic core already existed in the '90's, which has continued to showcase itself through wonderful offspring from those lines over the last twenty years. The GVHS as of this writing still holds to the idea that the Gypsy Vanner Horse is a type breed, whose genetic base is currently being built.

The amount of unexplained variety we are seeing both in the registered population as well as the unregistered population point to more genetic variability than should be found in a standardized breed; but is an understood component of a landrace. Yet, if you search and find those breeders who have remained focused on the older lines, once respected by the Gypsy families themselves, I believe you will see a genetic consistency that suggests a possible core. Could that be the elusive twenty percent the Thompsons spoke of when they introduced the Gypsy Vanner Horse breed? If you are a serious breeder, then I offer this as something to think about when making future breeding choices.

With a landrace, there is another reality that we have to come face to face with when determining if a breed exists. What if given the wide variety within the population and breeder choices, there was more than one group moving towards a level of genetic strength to classify as standardized breeds? The Gypsies didn't have to worry about this. They just lumped them all together and called them cobs. Breeders went whichever direction their likes or dislikes took them. No outside force to declare one right one wrong, one better than the other. However, after 1996 and the announcement that an actual breed now named Gypsy Vanner Horse could be identified within the population and the announcement shared not all of these cobs would qualify, then where are the Vanners and what are the others? As I began studying these horses it soon became clear there were two groups that had recognizably common traits but with clear differences especially in body. The Thompsons consistently shared the connection to the two Irish bred stallions, The Coal Horse and Sonny Mays. When we look at the herds coming out of Ireland in comparison to those from the British Gypsies in the 1990's we see a shift in body build. The Irish bred horses maintained a heavier build than did the British bred ones. I remember hearing Dennis Thompson share once when he was speaking of the mare, Shampoo Girl, the McCann family had told him to never sell this mare. The reason was she was a heavy mare and it would be important to breed back to her to keep the balance of body steady in their herd. It was about that thin line of balance. The herds that were producing the "Bok like horses" had moved ever so slightly away from the heavier cob type which could still be found in the Irish bred herds. The heavier herds had a much more draftier appearance while the horses which were being admired in England were slowly losing those elements, i.e. the less drafty head. Ultimately it was all about breeder preference, and clearly that takes us to today. There are breeders in the UK who have continued to breed the heavier horses and many of them are simply lovely. There are breeders here in the USA who believed heavier was the way to go and so we have them here as well. At the same time, we have these lovely herds of horses that meet that fine line of balance, possessing sufficient body thickness to be of the cob type, but whose build is less heavy enabling a more athletic and versatile ability. Both are registered in all of the current existing registries. However, the differences are such that at some point in time we as breeders and breed enthusiasts will have to face the question should they be classified as the same breed? Currently my research suggests two distinctly different possible breeds with a common ancestry. As we move forward and begin to sort through all of these important realities and connections I hope we make wise choices to preserve more than we eliminate.

Those of us who have been following these horses for some time continue to see a desired consistency in the twenty plus year breeding program at Gypsy Gold farm and in the breeding programs of others who sought out the genetics of the early horses and only brought in type horses to build on what they already respected. This supports what breed development research teaches us about growing a breed. While type based breeds certainly can be, and are enjoyed, and appreciated, they do not have a promise of a future. It is only the genetic based breed that can be maintained over time.

The educator in me realized this was not going to be a search to just understand a horse, but it was going to require me to understand cultures as well. I would need to get to know more about Gypsies; I would need to better understand the equestrian communities in both Ireland and England and question why they had not applauded this horse as a breed.

The answers would come. The Gypsies often could not read or write; much of the history of the early development of these lovely horses could only be found in the wonderful oral histories told by the aging men who had spent their lifetimes lovingly cultivating this new horse. Their pride and joy could be seen in their faces when a horse like Cushti Bok or my Bandit was shared at gatherings such as Appleby Fair.

As for the British and Irish equestrian communities, well, years and years of prejudice towards the Gypsy culture had blinded them to even the possibility that any Gypsy had any horse of real value. Therefore, this horse was simply not going to be recognized in its land of origin. It was going to take America to say, "I think you have something there; we like it; we want it; and we want to help you buy, sell, and trade it."

The difficulty came in the reality that this population was a landrace. Yet, with the establishment of the Gypsy Vanner Horse Society in 1996 there was now on the table the idea that a standardized breed existed. The problem: could the whole landrace be classified as this new breed, or just a portion of the landrace? Did the whole of the landrace have the potential to grow into this standardized breed? Even with these questions still unanswered for the bulk of the people now involved with these horses, at least this new community of horse lovers could agree that the following seven elements were what they wanted to see in their horses:

1. Short back in proportion to overall body (short distance between last rib to point of hip.)
2. Broad chest.
3. Heavy well-rounded hips (slab sided or severely sloping hindquarters are considered a fault.)

4. Heavy flat bone at the knee, ample hooves (small contracted hooves are considered a fault.)
5. Feathering that begins at the knees or near the hocks extending over the front of the hooves. Ample to abundant mane and tail.
6. Sweet head (fine head on a strong neck in harmony with the horse's overall look.)
7. Disposition (the horse should exhibit traits of intelligence, kindness and docility – overly aggressive behavior is considered a fault.)

(Brochure: A Colorful Combination/Thompson 2003)

The standard also included an element not found in other horse breeds. It suggested this new breed of horse could come in three distinct heights. Again, this would pose yet more questions. If you are recognizing a type with a strong genetic base, how can it come in three heights? Yet, the idea was certainly intriguing and made this group of horses even more unusual and desirable.

The circumstances surrounding the development of this group of colored horses, the mysterious culture whose breeding choices had created this population of animals, the struggles between cultures all became stumbling blocks to breed recognition.

The introduction of a group of these horses as a breed with a registry, a name, and a marketing plan, all in the age of the internet, set in motion a series of events that has been unmatched in the horse industry's history. It is by far a story filled with all the components of a good mystery story; it has all the elements of good vs. evil; and as you read on you will discover we are in the middle of it – with the end being unclear. The question still remains two decades into the drama, do we have a breed? If so, is it a genetic based breed or nothing more than a type of horse? Are the Gypsies responsible for the lovely horses, or is this now an American breed?

I know what I hope are the answers to these questions. For you the reader, read on. It is my wish to inspire you to search for truth, to use facts rather than opinions to give merit to your knowledge base, use respect and understanding for the genuine efforts of all who have made those for the sake of these lovely horses.

The next twenty years will be interesting I am certain; I only hope they take this lovely group of horses in a direction that respects them as well as the original Gypsy breeders, and the initial work done by the Thompsons to first at least make an effort to declare a portion of the landrace a breed.

In 1996 with the establishment of the Gypsy Vanner Horse Society by the Thompsons the Gypsy culture and its horses suddenly found themselves on the world stage. There was no turning back, now twenty plus years hence their fate is still to be determined.

CHAPTER
Four

A Brief History of Coloured Horses

When I first saw the beautiful Buck in a German riding school in 1995, there were Gypsies throughout the United Kingdom and for the most part all had and were breeding horses. As we have learned by the 1950's *coloured (British spelling used by Edward Hart in his work to denote these horses)* horses had become a status symbol for Gypsies. We have also found that originally the Gypsies had large draft crosses that were basically indiscriminately bred and in which color patterns may have occurred but were not dominant. Why and from where had these new herds of predominantly *"coloured* horses" come?

To answer our question, we must return to the work of Edward Hart. He tells us that *"colour"* meaning a broken coat; another color with white; had been around in many breeds for thousands of years. He even shares cave drawings have been found depicting horses of color. Mr. Hart quotes works by early equestrians such as Lady Wentworth in her *The World's Best Horses (1958),* in which she shares, "….skewbalds were common in Spanish horses in the Middle Ages and parti-coloureds of every conceivable pattern and shade are traditional in North Africa and even in Arabian history." Mr. Hart's work along with the work he shares from other *colour* enthusiasts is of great importance to us as we seek to understand the Gypsies' *coloured* horses.

According to the Thompson's study the Shire was an early contributing breed to our horses, so what did early *colour* enthusiasts have to say about this breed and its color preferences? In his work titled, *Horses Breeding to Colour (1912)* Sir Walter Gilbey shares that Mr. B. B. Colvin of Hertfordshire in the mid-nineteenth century had a group of piebald Shires on his farm that were breeding true (Hart 1993, 42). Typically, today we think of the Shire with a black body, white face blaze and white socks. Yet this history shares the broken coat was evidenced in this breed in the not too distant past. Also, given that our horses have a draft root I investigated *colour* in the Clydesdale. Here I found that the breed standard for this Scottish heavy horse prefers bay or brown with a white stripe on the face, legs white over the knees and hocks. I also learned that while the registry does not recognize piebald and skewbald as a Clydesdale *colour, of all modern heavies, the Clydesdales show unmistakable signs of overo markings. (Hart 1993,44)*

Given just these basic historical facts surrounding the Shire and Clydesdale which I believe we can safely say contributed to today's *coloured* horse from Gypsies I think it is obvious their beautiful broken coats had a genetic connection in these two draft breeds.

While it might be romantic to think so; there is little evidence to suggest that the Gypsies brought *coloured* horses with them when they first arrived in the British Iles. In fact, the research tends to indicate otherwise. The first Gypsies to the UK came as has been shared in bender tents with their work animal of choice being the donkey. Over time they adopted the living wagons and because they were poor they acquired horses which basically others would not have. These became their base stock. Many of these early horses were draft crosses chosen because of the job they had to do – pull a heavy load over great distances while maintaining demeanor even children could handle. The photo below from Dr. Hancock and Dr. Kyuchukov's book, *"A History of the Romani People"*, gives us a pictorial reference for the typical Gypsy's horse as of 1943.

Romanies were kept on the move all over Europe, especially during World War II. This group is winding through a town in 1943. Photo courtesy Dr. Ian Hancock.

The horses in the picture are indiscriminate, no tendency towards any recognizable, fashionable purebred at the time. This is pictorial evidence that Mr. Hart's facts bear out. If this photo is during the WWII time period and Mr. Hart shares by the 1950's *coloured* horses had become special to the Gypsies how then did they begin to gain herds of *parti-coloureds* quickly?

Equine geneticists will tell us that the tobiano pattern is dominant. Therefore, if a tobiano parent is bred to a solid color parent fifty percent of the foals from such a mating would be tobiano. According to a Gypsy, John Shaw, in the early 1950's Gypsies were crossing Dales and Fell pony mares with Clydesdale stallions. The stallions used were often roan with a lot of white, giving rise to a variety of colors. According to Mr. Shaw in the 1950's the Gypsies were using anything they could get their hands on. They could have been using the tobiano rule; a tobiano patterned horse, not breed specific bred to the offspring from the above mix might throw a tobiano foal with draft characteristics from the Clyde; while moving towards a smaller animal from the pony genetics infused through those pairings. Such a foal would then be prized and kept, the beginnings of the selectively bred herds of the 1990's.

Travellers in Ireland set up camp in a churchyard in County Galway just before a popular horse fair. Photo courtesy of the family of Mathias Opersdorff.

This photo from the work of Mathias Opersdorff, clearly shows a draft cross type horse in the foreground with two broken coat horses to the side. Each of these colored horses are lacking in today's desired conformation or hair attributes, but certainly bring their color to the mix. This is pictorial evidence of possibly one way the Gypsies were moving toward their new horse.

In the early stages of this process the Gypsies were producing the heavy *coloured* horses with excess mane, tail, and feathering. That makes sense in that their base stock would have been the large draft crosses making up the bulk of their herds during or near the end of WWII. But the larger the horse the more expensive to maintain and they were doing their best to move to a smaller more economical animal with the vision traits they had begun to admire. According to Mr. Hart, *".....for that you want the vanner type of 14.3 to 15 hands."* *(Hart 1993, 64)*

The Thompsons' research had led them to conclude the Gypsies had used predominantly Shires and Clydesdales, with the Dales Pony; all of these breeds have a heritage connection to the Friesian. If this is the case, then the recipe suggested by Mr. Hart was the beginning while as the selective herds grew and began to become a family's pride trait prominence could have been added or maintained through the introduction of the breeds listed in the Thompson study. No matter, it would be nearly impossible to outline specifically the breeds involved due to the indiscriminately bred crosses which formed the foundation. However, it is to these horses we owe the base for the tobiano and overo patterns and from older lines of the Shire and Clydesdale. In addition, we must recognize the contributions made by the variety of *coloureds* identified in multiple breeds and crosses found throughout the United Kingdom at the time the Gypsies began their breeding programs focused on creating herds of *coloured* horses.

Therefore, in the 1990's by the time of Mr. Hart's book (1993) and the Thompson discovery (1994-1996), herds of selectively bred *coloured* horses had become genetically uniform; had taken on a look and a set of traits all their own, but had gone unrecognized and uncelebrated outside of the Gypsy culture. In 1994 when Cushti Bok was first noticed, what did the total population of Gypsy bred *coloured* horses look like? To help us have a better idea of just how difficult the task of uncovering these purebred animals was please view the following chart:

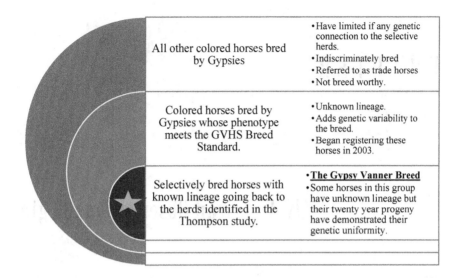

All other colored horses bred by Gypsies	• Have limited if any genetic connection to the selective herds. • Indiscriminately bred • Referred to as trade horses • Not breed worthy.
Colored horses bred by Gypsies whose phenotype meets the GVHS Breed Standard.	• Unknown lineage. • Adds genetic variability to the breed. • Began registering these horses in 2003.
Selectively bred horses with known lineage going back to the herds identified in the Thompson study.	• **The Gypsy Vanner Breed** • Some horses in this group have unknown lineage but their twenty year progeny have demonstrated their genetic uniformity.

In 1994 this total population of horses was approximately three to four thousand. Of that total, the Thompsons would learn from the Gypsies, only about six to eight hundred were the selectively bred horses (20% of the total *coloured* cob population) the Gypsies themselves had begun to admire.

If indeed, only 800 (let's use the larger end of the projection) horses were selectively bred then that would mean around 3,200 *coloured* horses would make up the remainder of the population of horses bred by Gypsies. If it is true Gypsies often hid their treasured horses (many stories have been shared regarding this practice) then you can begin to see why the British or Irish equestrian communities had overlooked the breed. They rarely, if ever, saw the selectively bred horses. We owe our gratitude to the Gypsy breeders who decided to breed selectively; who separated out their treasured horses, and then were willing to share them first with the Thompsons, and then with the many others who have followed over these last two decades.

CHAPTER
Five

My American Observations Begin

The journey to uncover the why, when, and how of this breed has been as you can see a fascinating one. When I acquired Magic and Bandit I knew this was a horse worth understanding and sharing. I was grateful to find the Thompsons and to learn of their accomplishments with the Gypsies. My experience had been with Gypsies who wanted to keep their privacy, sharing little if anything about the horses. Much like his colorful friends, Dennis kept his sources close. At first I was a bit angry with him. I could not understand why he just didn't broadcast who these breeders were and where they kept these wonderful selectively bred horses. It would take me five years and a meeting in Ohio to open my eyes.

Between 1998 and 2003 confusion had already started to be on the rise. If you have read the Thompson story on their website, you have learned of their special friendship with a respected Gypsy, Fred Walker. Mr. Walker's prediction that this was not going to be easy was becoming more and more validated with each passing year. I hate to say it, but I was completely oblivious to all the goings on. Rather I had moved to New York in 2001 bringing my beloved Magic and Bandit with me and had started to assist in helping introduce the breed at fairs and events in the northeast. My driving trainer, Susan Skipper, would tell me of a meeting for all owners of horses from Gypsies. This meeting would be just prior to the Ohio Equine Affaire in Columbus, Ohio in

2003. Susan had learned about this via the internet. This would be the beginning of my understanding of the role the internet would play in this breed's introduction. While the breed had been initially introduced by the Thompsons via their Gypsy Gold website in 1998 and then at Equitanna in Kentucky, the internet had now become a venue through which others would claim to own "the breed", give it other names, and begin to compete with, and even attempt to discredit, the Thompsons' work.

I made the trip to Ohio. I had done my homework and looked up several of the new websites for farms claiming to have these horses, under other names, and quoting Gypsies they now knew and called friends. Many of these individuals had learned of these horses first from the Gypsy Gold website and/or products, learned about a Gypsy horse fair, known as Appleby Fair, travelled there and started their own stories, most often giving no credit to the founding work of the Thompsons.

I want to be reasonable in my impression of all the early importers of horses bred by Gypsies and I include myself in that group. I found these horses and began to want to understand them prior to learning of the Thompson work; there may have been others who fall into this category as well. However, I believe we truly are an exclusive and extremely small group, none of which took the steps to establish a registry for these horses we were now beginning to appreciate. Sadly, it appeared to me these new owners and importers of horses from Gypsies wanted to take some or better yet all of the credit for uncovering the horses. From my viewpoint, it seemed many wished they had been the first to introduce the horses as a breed, rather than respecting the work already done and building on it. When I entered the conference area for this Ohio meeting the atmosphere was clearly one of vying for position – highly political and ready to ignite.

Remember the chart with the three circles in the previous chapter. Well, given the nature of the Gypsy culture, and the horse industry's driving force, horse trading, horses from all three circles now called America home under names like: Gypsy Vanner Horse, Gypsy Cob, Drum Horse, Colored Cob, Irish Tinker, Gypsy Horse. Were they all breed worthy as determined by the Thompson research? No. The answer here requires your definition of "breed". If you want to use an extremely loose interpretation and say the only qualifying attribute is "having a colored coat" then all the horses fit that description. On the other hand, if you used the Thompsons' more restrictive definition of "selectively bred heritage" and "specific conformational and behavioral attributes" set forth in their written standard then the answer would be, no. The division of horses bred by Gypsies as explained in the chart helps us define "the genetically uniform breed" which had been lifted out of the landrace and given one name, Gypsy Vanner Horse.

As I listened to these attendees explain and defend their positions my frustration grew. I held a much different perspective than most. My first encounter with horses from Gypsies had been in Germany when ordinary colored cobs had begun to be imported for riding stables due to their manageability and endurance. At that time, I had no knowledge of any efforts to recognize these horses as a breed, but was beginning to believe someone should do this. The horse that took my breath away was far from being "a common cob" had similarities yes, but those had long been much improved on. It was the breeding process that had brought the common cob to breed status that had intrigued me. Had caused me to observe and search to better understand the final product. That lead me to the Thompsons' research and joy over the breed and its now name, a title which along with the horse's unusual traits separated it from any and all other Gypsies' colored horses – Gypsy Vanner Horse – the centerpiece, one of the Gypsies' treasures.

As the conference progressed, I listened, and spoke when I felt I could make a positive contribution. It was obvious the task to get this group focused and working towards a consensus was going to prove more difficult than those who had planned this event imagined. It seemed the majority were there to make it somehow possible to successfully market any and all horses from Gypsies as something special; to bestow breed value and quality, though undeserved on the whole colored cob population. This was this teacher's first experience with business tactics and strategies; and a first-hand experience with horse trading at its best.

In the world of advertising and product promotion, I understood if I wanted a cola, I had a choice of soft drinks: Coca-Cola, Pepsi, and multiple imitations; I also knew Coca-Cola, "Coke" had started it all and still held traits setting it apart from the others. Somehow I felt the Gypsy Vanner must survive this colored cob invasion and come out in the end as the horse that started it all – an actual breed, and along with that recognition, an understanding of the quality only an original Gypsy Vanner Horse possesses in the ever- growing world of horses from Gypsies.

The meeting ended with a committee to look into the possibility of a single registry for all of these horses, and of course with the breed standard already set by the Gypsy Vanner Horse Society as the standard. This would never come to pass. Rather other registries would form to support the differences in opinion and the variety in the horses.

My heart was sad and my mind was spinning when I left Ohio. If you respect the standard of quality set by the Gypsy Vanner Horse Society then embrace it, get on board with the organization and purchase horses exhibiting the expected quality. At the Ohio meeting I had the opportunity to speak with Syd Harker and Michael Vines, two Gypsies attending as guests of those who planned the meeting. I would come to much respect the herds of Syd Harker as a founding selective herd and grow to appreciate Michael's desire to embrace and build the breed. I had shared photos of Magic and Bandit with them when they had asked how I knew so much about the horses. After taking a look Mr. Harker said, "You have a very good eye." That meant much to me coming from him.

Arriving back at home my concern was not so much about understanding the centerpiece of the breed as how to protect it. It would then occur to me that was the problem – no real understanding of a breed. No one was educating about the horse that held value for all of us. They were just trying to buy and sell horses – marketing vs. education. With the speed of the internet education had little chance to catch up.

Even Gypsy Gold had shifted. In 2002 with Cindy Thompson's death, naturally things changed. I personally feel Dennis has never recovered from that loss. It was a difficult couple of years for the registry and the breed. Dennis continued to do what he does best – market. However, the difference in his marketing and the marketing being done by all the others, many of whom I had met in Ohio was Dennis had the breed as he and Cindy had defined it; not at all saying the same quality was absent in horses imported by others. The difference – Dennis had imported and continued to import a limited number of horses; while others were continuing to mass import from a limited population of horses consisting of varied quality.

How then do we begin to help people want to better understand this population of colored cob horses? At some point, we have to stop "buying, selling, and trading" for a moment, and re-evaluate *what it is* we are "buying, selling, and trading". We have to be willing to become a community educated in breed recognition and development. In the case of these horses it is not only necessary, it is critical to first be willing to learn all that we can about the Gypsy culture and its history.

Was every Gypsy involved? Yes, to a degree. Most all Gypsies have horses and many breed horses. At the time after WWII for those who had horses and were breeding the main thing they wanted to do was to create a herd of horses unwanted by the government or outsiders. We have already determined that would be an all-white or mostly white horse; enter the broken coated horses, paint pattern, etc. Naturally the process began with what they already had – their large draft crosses. We would need to introduce white horses or broken coats into the mix. Next, if I start with large horses and I need the resulting product to be smaller I have to introduce smaller horses into the breeding plan. What better to do that than the local pony breeds/Dales, Fell, and others. The Thompsons have suggested the natural choice would have been the Dales Pony. It is a feathered breed and has a desired body type to compliment the direction they wanted to go.

While I believe, it would be somewhat impossible to find the exact horses that went into the process, I think it is safe to say each Gypsy family set out with what they had and knowing the desired traits made breeding choices in that direction. As with change of lifestyle on a group not all in the group become as enthusiastic as others about meeting new needs. There were a few men who set out to not only create a horse outsiders and the government would not want, but that would also make a statement about their family pride. All Gypsies were breeding for a smaller, mostly white, horse; all Gypsies continued to breed indiscriminately and extra horses were sold as commodity to the meat markets. However, the family pride group kept horses back, continued to improve on those, and within a twenty-year period had developed herds of horses the other families were noticing.

Cushti Bok became for the Thompsons the entry way into a culture's passion and the realization that what they had uncovered was a new breed. As they traced this little stallion's heritage, they met many of the families whose herds were the envy of their peers and began to know the names of the horses whose blood ran in Cushti Bok's veins and in the veins of all the other horses like him. These men maintained more than one herd. Their selective herd was the smaller of their herds and these horses were rarely, if ever, brought out into the open for anyone to see. Even at what would become the infamous Appleby Fair, they only brought good ones, keeping the best hidden. It would be only after it was clear that an interested party loved the horse and the look of the horse as much as the breeder himself, before an invitation would be issued to view the best he had to offer.

These men the Thompsons were getting to know *"had dedicated lifetimes to creating this horse"*. *(Thompson 1998)* It was not their desire to be known by the outside world, rather they did not believe their horses were for anyone except family and dear, dear friends. Their horses were a reflection of their family's pride, they were as colorful as the caravans they pulled, and they were a gift to them and therefore a gift to anyone with whom they chose to share them. This selectively bred group of horses had become the Gypsies' treasure.

Now in America what was happening? The original plan was to build the breed from the selectively bred herds. Yet mass importation had done the unthinkable; it had brought the whole of the *coloured* cob landrace to America and with the aid and speed of the internet the whole was being introduced as a breed.

CHAPTER
Six

Founding Fathers and Their Horses

N ow that you know the when, why, and how behind the Gypsy Vanner Horse, we need to discuss the actual men and their horses. After revealing more about the Gypsy way of life, the number of actual families breeding for quality, and the number of resulting horses I think we can all begin to see why Dennis and Cindy were so cautious. They have said they felt certain they would find many stallions of the same quality as Cushti Bok when they began their search. The truth of the matter was in the end they had only found two more: The Gypsy King and Romany Rye. Additionally, in the twenty plus years since the importing of the original sixteen horses to Gypsy Gold, Dennis has imported a limited number of horses, and all of those from the lines I will share later in this chapter. While during the same timeframe multiple farms have befriended many Gypsies, and imported many horses, I believe you can begin to see the pattern here.

If as the chart previously shared clearly outlines we were dealing with a total of three to four thousand colored horses and of that total only about eight hundred (20% of the population) were the Gypsies' selectively bred herds, we can certainly see the problem in identifying the men and their horses. Also, we have to take into account the Gypsy culture's opinion of outsiders. This treasured horse was not even for their fellow Gypsies (remember they often hid them), why then would they even consider sharing these bloodlines with outsiders – truthfully, it is unthinkable from where they sat.

The Thompsons shared they could not purchase all the horses they wanted to at the time they found them. The Gypsies were not parting with the horses they considered their best. It became about negotiation, waiting, waiting, and waiting some more. In fact, it took two years to negotiate the purchase of their beloved second stallion, The Gypsy King.

The question remains who were the men and who were the horses that made up that starred center circle and were no more than approximately six to eight hundred at the time of their discovery? Let us start with the names of the men as I have come to know their horses over the last two decades. First of course was **Roy Evans**, who owned Cushti Bok at the time he was discovered by Dennis and Cindy. Through Cushti Bok, we would learn about his breeder, **Tom Price.** We would learn that the **Connors** had raised Cushti Bok's sire, The Old Horse of Wales, and sold him to Tom Price. Mr. Price had several herds of horses and when he showed the Thompsons and other future American buyers his horses of course he shared his selective herd whose stallion was, The Old Horse of Wales. Then there was **Fred Walker**, the mentor and friend of the Thompsons, and known to his peers as *The King of the Coloured Horses*, a title bestowed upon him because during his lifetime he had owned many of the founding stallions and mares in what would become the breed.

The Thompsons' work and the work of many of us that followed would reveal that almost all of the selective herds had their roots in two Irish bred stallions Sonny Mays and The Coal Horse. Through the Thompsons, Jan Anderson, Lise McNamara, Jeff Bartko (all early American importers) and others we soon knew of the McCann family. **Patsy McCann** had spent his lifetime dedicated to breeding the perfect caravan horse. His son, **Jimmy McCann**, would tell the story of their herd's foundational stallion, Romany Rye, and share his father's legacy. In their search for quality horses to lay the foundation of this new breed the Thompsons would visit Appleby Fair and meet **Tom Draper** who owned a stallion named, Bill. They would later acquire Bill and change his name to The Gypsy King.

In 2003 I would be asked to provide an introduction to the Gypsy Vanner Horse for the New Jersey State Fair. In the process of developing that program, I would meet Lise McNamara and learn she owned a McCann bred mare that had been bred to Cushti Bok. I would visit her farm, encourage her to register her horses with the Gypsy Vanner Horse Society and learn about and fall in love with the wonderful horses from the **Robert Watson** and **John Pratt** breeding programs that had come to America primarily through Jan Anderson. Watson and Pratt grounded their breeding program in a particular stallion's bloodline, the The Roadsweeper UK who was a son of The Coal Horse. I loved the elegant, yet sturdy build of the Watson/Pratt horses. Also, connected to The Coal Horse was another of his sons known as **Eddie Alcock's** The Old Black Horse. This horse would be bred to the Crimea Mare producing a mare Robert Watson loved, The Teddy Mare. This mare and her daughters were imported and have produced incredible foals at Lise McNamara's farm, Blarney Stone Acres. Eddie's Old Black Horse would also sire a stallion that came to be known as **Amos Wiltshire's** Old Horse Sam. He would in turn produce a beautiful contributing stallion registered as Westmoreland The Lottery Horse. I began to spend much time reviewing websites and looking at the horses coming into America and trying to identify the herds and horses of respected breeders.

Frequently I would come across the name **Henry Conners** and grew to appreciate what his Old White Horse and later the stallion, Young Henry Connors brought to the breed while recognizing it was from the Connors lines Cushti Bok had come. Henry Connors White Horse would also sire a stallion known as The Lob Eared Horse. This Connors based stallion would also become famous as a contributing sire to the Gypsy Vanner Horse breed. I would learn that **Josey Conners** had bred a stallion named, The Lion King, out of a mare known as the PO Mare. This stallion would become a recognized and respected foundation sire to the Gypsy Vanner Horse breed. In 2003 I would as I have shared have the opportunity to meet **Sydney Harker** whose mares

I had already come to admire. It was those mares that taught me about their sire, Sid's Good Stallion, and his wonderful offspring.

In 2003 Dennis Thompson, would import a stallion Cindy had much loved and wanted to bring to America. Again, it was about waiting and sadly this beautiful horse did not arrive until after her death. Yet, he is a tribute to her recognition of what the breed was and should always be, the stallion in England had been called King Arthur, and Cindy had wanted to name him, Latcho Drom which means "Safe Journey". So, it was that this beautiful stallion, owned at the time of purchase by **Andrew Moulden**, would make a "safe journey" and come to Gypsy Gold adding his powerful genetics to the process of preserving and building this breed.

I am so proud to own a Latcho Drom grandson, who is also a Cushti Bok grandson. This wonderful Mark J. Barrett photo is of my stallion, VV Mayacamas. The blood of so many of the foundation horses runs in his veins to include not only Latcho and Bok but also: GG Rose, Shampoo Girl, Romany Rye, The Old Horse of Wales, The Lion King, The Lob Eared Horse, The Roadsweeper UK, Sonny Mays and The Coal Horse.

While the names I have mentioned are few, they are the men whose horses have continued to capture my attention in the two decades I have been on this journey. The list is certainly small in number as are the herds of horses they raised. In the last couple of years as the number of horses coming to America has grown I have been even more conscious of these bloodlines. These foundation horses set the bar of quality; that bar can so easily be lowered by the elements of horse trading: breeding up, cross breeding, all to generate business; not to protect or preserve a breed.

Those who have carefully followed these horses since their introduction, have a responsibility to educate people becoming involved with the breed as well as the general public about the bloodlines the Gypsies themselves treasured. Those bloodlines have already begun to prove who they are; consistency in quality progeny; excellence in attributes. Yet, it remains our responsibility to intentionally educate about who the families were and to name the bloodlines they left us. Many of these men are no longer alive, this is their legacy, their gift, and it should be the duty of those who love the breed to respect and honor what we have been given.

CHAPTER
Six

Part II

In the first part of this chapter I have given you the names, in my opinion, of the most highly respected original Gypsy breeders. It was the horses these men owned, bred, or sold to other Gypsies and to us that laid the foundation for the selective herds that caused heads to turn in the 1990's. With that said we need to start taking a closer look at the horses. Let's start at the beginning. The research done by the Thompsons and others concluded that the selective herds could be traced back to two Irish bred stallions – Sonny Mays and The Coal Horse. *(Starred (*) horses in the outlines below indicate the original sixteen imports and are recorded as numbers 1-16 in the Gypsy Vanner Horse Society registry.*

Sonny Mays
>The Sham
>>Fantasia
>>>Queen Nala of Feathered Gold
>>Henry Connors
>>>Smokey

The PO Stallion
The PO Mare
The Lion King
Young Henry Connors
Mr. Biker Connors N'Co

The Irish Blagdon Mare
The Lob Eared Horse
Vardo Joe
*Esmeralda
Bob the Blagdon
Flash
Gypsy Gold's Rose
Blossom's Filly
The Road Sweeper
Daughter of the Lob
Sid's Good Stallion aka The Frainy Horse

The Coal Horse
The Roadsweeper UK
Bonnie UK
*Imari
The Black Face Mare
Charlie
Robert Watson's Old Horse/Tom/Lad
Blarney Stone's Sailor
Babes

The Original Old Paddy
The Horseshoe Mare
Bob the Blagdon
Shogun
The Vincent Mare

Eddie Alcock's The Old Black Horse
The Kuchi Stallion
Lakeridge British Sterling
Amos Wiltshire's Old Horse Sam
Westmoreland's The Lottery Horse
Royal
The Teddy Mare

While this is certainly not a complete list of offspring, it is what I see as a strong beginning if you will. The horses listed here have made significant contributions to furthering consistency in the breed to date. In addition, we have the following contributing stallions that warrant inclusion in such a distinguished group.

The Original Kent Horse
Shogun
Tubbs
Black Beard

The Old Horse of Wales
*Cushti Bok (Recognized as the first Gypsy Vanner Horse Stallion)
*Cushti Bok Lady (the only imported daughter of Cushti Bok)
Romany King
Shampoo Boy

*The Gypsy King – This foundation stallion began his USA breeding career in the 1998 season producing America's first born Gypsy Vanner Horse, the mare, Kuchi, out of the McCann bred mare, *Bat. His daughter, *Darby Dolly, along with *Bat were the first two Gypsy Vanner Horses to set foot on American soil. In addition, among the original imports were four other daughters from this outstanding stallion:

*King's Kaulo Ratti
*Gypsy Gold's Rexi

*King's Gypsy Princess
*Crown Darby

Romany Rye - each of the following mares sired by this outstanding stallion became five of the original imported horses to lay the foundation for the Gypsy Vanner Horse breed in America.

*Bat
*Jasmine
*Chauvani
*Shampoo Girl
*Romany's Ms. Bodi

Latcho Drom – This foundation stallion began his USA breeding career in 2003, producing in his first season:

1234 Filly
Latcho Drom's Caymus
Latcho's Gypsy Lass
Magnolia's Sparkle

While without question breeds tend to highlight stallions in their pedigrees we must not forget the other half of that equation. The following contributing mares and their offspring warrant being acknowledged when seeking to respect a core in this breed.

The PO Mare
The Lion King

The Wagon Mare
The Midget Mare
Miss Downs
Oakfield Miss Minnie
May (aka) Muddy

The Horseshoe Mare
> Bob the Blagdon
> Shogun
> The Boss UK
> The Vincent Mare

The Irish Blagdon Mare
> The Lob Eared Horse

The Crimea Mare
> The Teddy Mare
>> My Wild Irish Rose
>> Teasel
>> Westmoreland Teddy Girl
>> Clannad

Old Rose
> The Rose
>> Some of this mare's most recognized foals were by Sid's Good Stallion:
>>> WR Panda Rose
>>> Prince Charming
>>> Tessa Rose
>>> BFS Gypsy Rose
>> Since arriving in America she was bred to other outstanding stallions continuing to build this line.

*Papuza – this mare was one of the original sixteen imports and while her sire's and dam's lineage were unknown she has definitely left her mark on the foundation of the Gypsy Vanner Horse breed through her outstanding offspring which include:

> Equirace Gypsy
> Vanilla Swirl

Vintage Vanners Bommarito
Vintage Vanners Carmanet Time
Chakano
Maximus

To attempt to name and honor a core for any breed is a monumental undertaking. The point is it is work that must be done. In all established breeds, we find the foundational pedigrees that marked the beginning of such genetic based groups. In chapter ten I will share a bit of the Thoroughbred story with you. In that story, it is clear that three, only three stallions are honored by Thoroughbred breeders as their beginning.

I believe the Thompsons envisioned the original sixteen imports as the Gypsy Vanner Horse breed beginning, while respecting their connection to Sonny Mays and The Coal Horse. However, with Cindy's death, and the many political shifts within the Gypsy Vanner Horse Society, that vision got sidetracked. As of this writing no official acknowledgement of a core genetic group has been declared by the GVHS. Rather, the idea is presented that all horses currently registered are the beginning of the foundational core for the breed. That group is approximately five thousand.

I hope you realize that such a number could not realistically represent a core. Therefore, my goal was to at least name some of the horses that I have encountered both personally, through their offspring, or through verbal history stories shared that have captured my attention because of who they are, what they look like, and what they have produced.

For me the Gypsy Vanner Horse will always be the 1996 model; people will and have changed it; but the horses I have named embraced it. We all have our preferences, but when recognizing a breed, we have to come to some standard of consensus and see the bloodlines that produced that standard before it became the standard.

CHAPTER
Seven

What's in A Name?

I want to return to the "name thing" just one final time and attempt to without prejudice, outline what had happened, did happen, and is now happening. At the beginning of this book you read a rather passionate plea to support the name Gypsy Vanner Horse. Now that you have read and learned more about the Gypsies and their horses we should now return to the topic of a breed name and consider its importance in the process of breed recognition.

I cannot stress enough the adjectives rare and few with regards to this colored cob population living throughout the United Kingdom in the 1990's. We will begin with the people responsible for these lovely animals, the Gypsies. Historically, this culture had owned and bred horses primarily for transportation. These people also as a culture had a genuine admiration for the horse. There was pride in horsemanship. The ability to demonstrate a skilled relationship with the animal was respected within the community. This was tradition. I believe it was this cultural understanding and love of the horse that was behind the breeding decisions which ultimately would create the colored cob horses.

By the 1970's the need for the large pulling horses was gone. Also, traveling in their wagons was now more ceremonial than lifestyle. While there were forces outside their control which had changed their lifestyle, those forces could not diminish their love of the horse.

It is here that I must throw in a little bit of mystery, magic, and romance – after all this is the Gypsy culture we are discussing. This is a culture choosing to remain separate from the cultures with which they shared countries. There is a mystery here. Why not become immersed in the culture where you have found a place to live? Why hold on to old customs? Tracing the people who have become known as Gypsies over their thousand-year history reveals that no matter where they lived, they remained Gypsies. Though eventually being recognized as citizens of their respective new countries, they still held firm to who they were and from where they had come. They had boundaries, though invisible to the locals, which kept the outsiders at a proper distance. If you read their stories, and enjoy the poetry that has embraced their ideals you will find that these people see the world as their country. It was life on the open road that still had deep roots in their hearts. People who settle and establish a homestead find their blessings in what they see as security and a place of their own. The Gypsy sees those same blessings as hindrances to adventure and the opportunity to experience what lies just over the next hill.

Learning and respecting these truths about these people helps us to begin to better understand their breeding choices which would create these new horses. By the 1980's the Gypsy culture had successfully bred broken coats into the bulk of the horses they owned and raised. The cob body type had been infused into a percentage of the population, but remained a small portion. While color pattern, piebald being the preferred, was apparent and primary, conformation was variable throughout the herds; ranging from large to pony size animals with varying builds and abilities. Again, how many animals are we discussing? A total suggested number has been from three to four thousand. I believe one of the most difficult hurdles to get over for Americans is their inability to grasp what this incredibly small number of animals meant in the 1990's and continues to mean for us as owners and breeders today in 2018.

We live in a world where breeds exist in rather large numbers, usually in the hundreds of thousands. In that world, experimental breeding: crossbreeding for performance, colors, size changes, is of little threat to the population as a whole. Actually, such experimentation is sometimes embraced and even encouraged. In reality we cannot afford to overlook what those choices could and would do to a population numbering only a few thousand animals.

Therefore, anyone coming across this population in the 1990's with a sincere interest to understand it, first recognized the fragile number. A serious horseperson would without question next recognize the obvious variety within the group. There would be a need to find the consistencies as well as the variables and then determine the next steps for conservation and preservation, if the group was of any importance.

What drives the horse industry? The buying, selling, and trading of horses is what makes the industry an industry. Therefore, whether these horses offered something worth selling would determine just how important they were to the outside world. Was this important to the Gypsy culture? For some, naturally, for the culture as a whole I have to say my research suggests whether they could sell horses was not of utmost importance to them; I believe what was of greatest importance to the Gypsy was the ability to keep horses in his life. As a result, by the 1990's most Gypsy breeders were meticulously downsizing their herds to the pony size. Why? With less and less land available to them for grazing their herds, they needed to have smaller animals which could survive on smaller pasture areas; even in a backyard if need be.

As the 1990's drew to a close, most Gypsies had begun to admire and appreciate the colored cob type horses, and they called them Coloured Cobs. Within this group which they had successfully maintained the color pattern and the cob body type, there still existed variety. These horses had attracted some attention from the British who began to enjoy the color in this population. In fact, Edward Hart's book, *"The Coloured Horse and Pony"*, discusses how color enthusiasts had formed "Coloured Horse Clubs", not breed specific, to celebrate the broken coats. Therefore, the British began referring to these horses as Gypsy Colored Cobs, or Gypsy Cobs. Again, there was no real delineation of quality; they embraced them all tall, short, heavy, light. As neighboring countries began to show an interest the horses soon had yet another label, that of Gypsy Horses and from Germany they added Tinker

Horse. All of these terms embraced the whole of the colored horse population. Truthfully, there is absolutely nothing wrong with that, in fact it makes perfectly good sense given the extremely small number of animals.

All of these early enthusiasts certainly liked these horses. However, there is no record of any of them thinking about any future for these animals. Culturally, why would they? Historically, all of these people understood that Gypsies breed horses, and that those horses change over time because that is what Gypsies do; they experiment and create. None of those cultures saw the need to intervene on behalf of these newly enjoyed horses and by the late '90's ponies as well.

If no one had stepped up to the plate and intentionally decided to determine if any of these animals could be classified as a type breed or better yet a genetically based breed, what could have happened?

Given the geography, and if breeding had remained within the Gypsy community, we would have a beautiful population of colored cob type ponies numbering less than five thousand, being enjoyed within the Gypsy culture in the UK. There would remain a few horse size animals due to the varying preferences of the individual breeders, i.e. those who still breed for the trotting horses. While in Ireland those personal preferences would have continued to support the heavier cob horses and ponies. The numbers in general would have remained small due simply to the geographical boundaries as well as the cultural ones.

Here again we have to turn to mystery, magic, and romance to get our minds around what would happen. It would take America with its cultural love of diversity, its understanding of breeds, and its appreciation for structure to protect those breeds, to see the beauty and potential in this unrecognized group of animals. With the establishment of the Gypsy Vanner Horse Society in 1996 the first effort to move in that direction had been put in motion.

In 1998 Americans saw and then questioned what is a Gypsy Vanner Horse? While it was, the first-time most Americans were seeing, and wondering about these horses, this certainly was not the case for the peoples of the United Kingdom, and more importantly the Gypsies themselves, and these folks did not call these horses Gypsy Vanner Horses.

If you read the discovery story shared by Dennis and Cindy Thompson via their website www.gypsygold.com, the first thing you will notice is that they point out immediately that the Gypsy Vanner Horse is a horse found in small numbers within the population of colored cobs. I have always remembered a quote from Cindy Thompson, "All Vanners can be Cobs, but not all Cobs can be Vanners."

She was saying there are a few thousand colored cobs in the United Kingdom, but they don't all possess the quality, the identified traits, that have been selectively bred into some of the herds, to classify them as a type and more importantly a genetic based breed. The ones that do possess those requirements can be a standardized breed and they needed a name. As a result of studying this culture and the horses it created over several years, and after working closely with some of the culture's leading and most respected breeders, and seeking their approval the Thompsons chose a name for this extremely small group of animals. The name is Gypsy Vanner Horse.

Up until that moment in time all of the horses and ponies were referred to as cobs.

Breed development research teaches us that there has to be a time when someone, a group of folks, somehow take a serious look at an animal population, and declare the group a breed either because it can reproduce one trait, or multiple traits within its offspring. Without this structure those traits more than likely will be lost over time. That research takes us further along the continuum of breed stability by stating that to only be recognized by type cannot guarantee consistency in progeny; it is only the group that demonstrates a genetic base which consistently reproduces type that has a chance at being maintained for the future.

Therefore, the name Gypsy Vanner Horse is critical when it comes to breed recognition for these horses. It was chosen to name the Thompsons' suggested twenty percent of the colored cob population that possessed a forty-year genetic history as of the 1990's and was consistently reproducing the desired traits in offspring. The name

Gypsy Vanner Horse was never intended for the whole of the colored cob population. And if I might say, Cindy Thompson's quote suggests, therefore just because a horse can be labeled cob does not qualify it as a Gypsy Vanner Horse. While this should have been nothing more than an understood delineation, it became a vicious political battle which has done harm to the recognition of these horses as a respected breed.

The founding of multiple registries all suggesting a variety of breed names: Gypsy Cob, Gypsy Horse, Gypsy Pony, etc. has not been in the best interest of any of these animals, at least that is what a study into long respected breeds tells us.

Culturally Americans like to be first; they like to be winners. These cultural traits have also played parts in where we are today with the colored cob horses from the Gypsies. Through mass importation of the entire population of colored cob type horses, many of which did not meet the standard outlined by the Thompsons in their work, naturally all those other labels had to come into play for any horse not meeting the GVHS standard. People owning such horses then considered themselves first in setting up other registries, using the old labels, and suggesting time and time again that by doing so they somehow were honoring the Gypsy culture.

While the Gypsy Vanner Horse Society has been able to continue, the journey has not been an easy one as you have and will read in this work. The important part of this chapter is for you to begin to understand that the name, Gypsy Vanner Horse, is important as the marker for breed recognition. A group of horses was studied, and given the traits this group exhibited at the time of recognition, a breed standard was recorded, and a breed name was carefully chosen. This became the beginning of a structured organization whose purpose was breed recognition and then breed preservation.

What is in a name? For a new breed, it is a reward; it is recognition finally received; it is a historical marker; it becomes a label for quality determined by a standard. It honors those who made the breeding choices leading to this group of remarkable animals, and respects those efforts as founding ones. It calls attention to this accomplishment and becomes an announcement to the world that this animal is here.

While the modern-day Gypsy may not have the ability to continue to travel the world in his horse drawn colorful caravans, his masterpiece, his treasured and most beloved horses and ponies are making the journey for him. They are being discovered by horsemen and horsewomen who are experiencing the unique and admirable traits that only the mystery and magic of the Gypsy culture could have envisioned. As of this writing the community of horse people worldwide still have the job of coming to consensus on the names. In the midst of that discussion is the name that caused heads to turn towards a culture and their horses for the first time ever – that name is and will always remain a vital part of this history – Gypsy Vanner Horse. What the industry does with this gift remains a question.

CHAPTER
Eight

Changes on the Rise

The Gypsy Vanner Horse Society was started in 1996. It has since that time gone through growth trends. The first shift occurred in 2003 following the Ohio meeting, when Mr. Thompson opened the registry to not only "center circle" horses, but the best of the "second circle" as well (See chart in Chapter Four). In 2004 with the help of a business partner, Doug Kneis, he agreed to allow the GVHS to become a non-profit breed organization being overseen by a Board of Directors. With this new format in place, the Society was now democratic.

This was an appropriate move when you look at the total number of horses bred by Gypsies; the breeding practices of those Gypsies; and the horses within the population that are connected genetically. Equine geneticists agree within a horse population it is wise to include specimen of unknown pedigree whose phenotype and characteristics resemble the standard set for the breed. This expands the genetic base and is healthy for the longevity of the breed.

This process works for the health and growth of the breed when those unknown horses are bred back to complimentary pedigreed horses. The resulting offspring can then be bred to horses with unknown lineage or back again to core genetic animals depending upon the quality of the horses. Always including or choosing animals reflecting the quality outlined in the breed standard and found in original pedigrees should be the plan of successful breeders. Given the extremely small number of respected pedigrees at the time of discovery, it is crucial for breeders to expand and build those families of horses. The problem resulting from mass importation, without any structured education program to help new buyers understand breed recognition and development, let alone cultural differences, is that many breeders have bred unknown horses to unknown horses thereby growing a large population of horses without the quality expected in the breed when it was first recognized. In addition, by 2005 there had begun to be an interest in horses from Gypsies of colors other than the expected piebald and skewbald patterns. Suddenly palomino, buckskin, and even appaloosa patterns began to appear in horses from Gypsies. While the GVHS breed standard stated the Gypsy Vanner was "not a color breed" within the known pedigrees the colors had been consistent: piebald, skewbald, and understood and accepted variances of those known colors. If so, where were these unusual colors coming from, who was breeding them, and why was there an interest in moving away from the original color palette?

America will always want something new, something different. Gypsies will always buy, sell, and trade horses as a profitable profession. This breed as originally introduced was in jeopardy of changing due to these cultural behaviors. It didn't matter that in 2005 efforts were being made to first understand "what the breed was" and then once understood, protect and build that breed. No, most of these folks saw any and all horses coming from Gypsies as a breed and if the horse was not a color breed then why not a horse of a different color?

The problem: crossbreeding and diluting an already scarce population of purebred animals. Any credible equine geneticist will tell you in order to get some of these odd color combinations you would have to step away from the breed to do so – crossbreeding. The Gypsy Vanner Horse Society had always discouraged crossbreeding. Yet, due to the fact the breed standard did not specify which colors were acceptable, the GVHS found itself having to accept these odd colored horses whose phenotype met the breed standard. From my observations, the problem has been in the resulting foal crops. In some cases, these odd colored horses do not consistently reproduce their colors in their offspring. Therefore, what I am seeing is that many of the resulting foals have a watered down, murky look to their color pattern and many times do not possess the other expected traits – desired conformation, amount of bone, mane, tail, and feather, etc.

What is important for us to understand is that the Gypsy Vanner Horse, the small portion of the landrace intended by the Thompsons as the breed, was not recognized on color alone. Rather it was the whole package, the combined attributes that drew those of us in the early years of recognition to these horses. At that time piebald was the prize, but it came with a beautiful head, sufficient mane, tail, and feather to expand its beauty, as well as an uncanny intelligence for a horse, a docility that caused wonder, and a movement that set it apart.

Due to crossbreeding to obtain some of these newer color combinations we simply are not seeing the whole package in many of these newer, more recent bloodlines. That is not to say this cannot be reached by these breeders who have become so enamored with these new colors. What I want us to realize is that it took Gypsy men with plan and purpose behind their selective breeding forty plus years to achieve the whole package in piebald. In my humble opinion, it will take at least that long to achieve it in these newer colors.

If you are one of these hopefuls, don't give up on your dream, stay focused and committed to the quality in the original piebalds, then move in that direction though be it now in a different color. In the meantime, be truthful about your efforts and their results; make wise choices within the population of odd color, choosing from the strongest phenotypes, and knowing when you can the genetic history, even at which generation the new color was first introduced. Making solid breeding choices from the original foundation horses – the core, if you will to move your herd towards excellence.

As of 2018, we find ourselves failing to grow as a community. There remains a general loss of respect for the name, Gypsy Vanner Horse, with the term, Gypsy Horse, being used most frequently by the open market. Therefore, farms wishing to simply buy and sell horses continue to say "the horses are all the same" and state that all the names are simply labels for the same horses. A small percentage of interested buyers are slowly beginning to connect the title, Gypsy Vanner Horse, with the look and traits associated with those original horses establishing the breed and its registry.

A quick review of websites, and internet forums, about these horses will reveal that at present despite the registries, breeders appear to be more interested in various phenotypes (thick drafty and thinner more athletic) and odd colors rather than original pedigrees which produced desired phenotypes. What does this mean for the Gypsy Vanner Horse breed's future? I fear it means a loss of quality and a steady move away from the genetics that created the horse I came to know and love; that the Gypsies themselves treasured; that the Thompsons' recognized as a breed; and that captured America's interest when introduced from 1996 to 1998.

How can this trend of moving away from the founding herds be directed back to treasured bloodlines? We need to name the horses and the men behind the horse, we need to acknowledge that crossbreeding is being done to acquire odd colors, and we need to be educated about how to build a solid genetic base by breeding first consistently within core bloodlines, then out to acceptable unknown horses within the registry, then those foals back to known bloodlines until we have a strong group of horses that will carry on the vision of the men behind the horse – it all started after all with a focus on desired phenotype and the bloodlines consistently producing that phenotype - a passion for pedigree.

CHAPTER
Nine

Performance and the Gypsy Vanner Horse

O nce we establish the horse with its amazing attributes that is the breed, then we must ask the question what can this wonderful, new breed of horse do? What will its contributions to the horse industry be?

We know the Gypsy Vanner gets its name from its original intent which was the perfect caravan horse. Twenty years following its introduction it has successfully lived up to that expectation. It is an amazing and beautiful driving horse.

I love this old photo of me driving my Bandit. It was taken during our training time together. Bandit was teaching me to drive. I say that because my trainer, Susan Skipper,

and I were both blown away at Bandit's innate and natural ability when it came to this discipline. In time as I got to know other owners the story was always the same, it was as if these horses were born knowing how to be driving horses.

The Gypsy Vanner Horse or if we like shorten the name to Vanner, has in its brief history astonished both newcomers as well as long time professionals at its ability to perform many equine disciplines with ease. I shared with you my first encounter with the horses at a German riding stable where they had been growing in popularity as comfortable riding mounts. They made excellent partners for beginning riders due to their calm and manageable temperament. The horses were well suited for overnight trail rides as well as a trustworthy mount in the many riding classes offered at the riding school.

Once we arrived in America we soon found not only were the Vanners beautiful under English tack; they also could take on the Western world giving it a colorful new addition. Shortly after coming to the USA my daughter and the West Point equestrian coach, Sherry Cashman, trained our Bandit to perform the single barrel dash for a collegiate show. We were going to bring him just so people could see this new breed, but my daughter insisted he had to enter at least one class. Amazingly he took second place beating out experienced Quarter Horses.

Over the years it has been fun to watch the list of accomplishments grow for this breed. They have begun to prove themselves in dressage, trail, hunter/jumper competitions, roping and reining events. Basically, the breed has demonstrated a willingness and an intelligence to learn multiple disciplines and are consistently pleasing their new owners with the levels they can achieve.

While a wide performance base means a good, steady market for the future of the Gypsy Vanner Horse I see a more valuable contribution yet unrealized for these horses. As an educator, I believe one of their greatest contributions may be in the area of equine assisted education and therapy. In both New York and Louisiana, my Gypsy Vanner Horses and I had the opportunity to work with a small number of children with disabilities. It was clear to the teachers and parents and myself that these horses have an uncanny sense of perception when it comes to the people in their lives; they seem to sense needs and know how to build a relationship to help heal. They are intelligent, willing, calm and manageable; all the traits desired in a therapy horse. Such programs typically rely on older horses who are less of a fright and flight risk; resulting in a lower liability environment. Younger horses tend to be a greater risk and usually are not chosen for this reason. However, with the older horses they no sooner are trained than many die, leaving a void in the program and often a long wait for a replacement. Enter the Gypsy Vanner Horse who as early as four years of age can serve therapy programs and successfully provide a safe environment to grow healthy, healing relationships that can be ongoing for many years. When Sue Rathbone, owner of El Brio Stables decided to downsize she chose to donate some of her Vanners to therapy programs. In the 2013 issue of The Vanner Magazine, official publication for the Gypsy Vanner Horse Society, the following story was shared by Jeanna Pellino of Hidden Acres Therapeutic Riding Center in Naugatuck, Connecticut:

It takes a very special horse to be part of the Hidden Acres therapy herd as they must possess a gentle and patient spirit, most typically found in older horses. However, the youngest member of our herd at four years of age is Gypsy Vanner EB Kendall Jackson. Kendall was donated to Hidden Acres in December 2012 by Sue Rathbone of El Brio Stables, to honor the victims of Sandy Hook Elementary School and to serve those traumatized by the event. A favorite of all who visit the farm, it is not only Kendall's beauty that attracts children like a magnet with her striking black and white body, and her long flowing forelock and mane, but it's what's inside her – a soul so gentle and sensitive it instinctively draws people in. As soon as she sees a visitor, she'll come right to the stall door, turn and press her mane against it, so the child or adult may stroke her. You can see any tension in the individual melt away as Kendall works her equine magic just being herself-a gentle, loving soul. (The Vanner Magazine. Rathbone/Pellino 2013, 11)

We are just now beginning to build the research reflecting the Gypsy Vanner's high level of success in these much-needed programs addressing the many needs of today's society.

In addition, the Gypsy Vanner has captured a yet untapped market for the horse industry; older, first time horse owners. At the time of the introduction of this breed, there existed a group of Baby Boomers, who had a love of horses but had never become horse owners. Many because of their age, and fear of an animal with a fright and flight risk. Also, popular breeds prior to the Gypsy Vanner tended to be larger horses, over fifteen hands. The size alone was a deterrent for these hopeful horse lovers. Suddenly they met a fairytale horse, colorful and enchanting, a horse they had only dreamed about standing somewhere between fourteen and fifteen hands. A horse that was sweet, manageable, and possessing an intelligence capable of communicating its desire to be a willing and safe partner.

The Gypsy Vanner is just beginning its life as a respected and much sought after breed. With its wide range of abilities, I foresee it becoming a horse with a unique and expanding future – a horse people will want, use, and enjoy in many ways to enrich and build lives.

CHAPTER
Ten

Building the Gypsy Vanner
Breed Through its Registry

Recently as part of my research I began to look at how other breed registries took form. The Thoroughbred for instance was founded primarily on the bloodlines of three known stallions, The Byerley Turk, The Darley Arabian, and The Godolphin Arabian. Initially there were no written records for these horses and information was kept by individual breeders or passed down by word of mouth. In addition, it was difficult to trace some of these horses because Thoroughbreds were not named until they had proved themselves on the racetrack. Then a gentleman by the name of James Weatherby conducted his own research and compiled a collection of private pedigree records to build the first General Stud Book. What is fascinating is the quality produced by those founding bloodlines continues to be evident in the great horses as this breed has grown. The Jockey Club has managed to protect its beloved breed from a top down management which has limited the interference of a democratic human element.

Currently the Gypsy Vanner Horse is still so very young. The process that created it is approximately seventy years old with its recognition as a breed only twenty years old as of this writing. We are just beginning to build this incredible breed on the foundation of the selective herds of the original Gypsy breeders. When Dennis and

Cindy Thompson chose the three original stallions, I believe they were following the Thoroughbred plan. Those stallions had come from truly selective breeding programs and had themselves already been proven as sires prior to their selection to lay the foundation for the Gypsy Vanner Horse in America. Of course, Romany Rye did not come to America but his daughters became his representatives and contributors. Twenty years into this process I still see the power of those genetics in the Gypsy Vanner Horses being born from those lines today. The Thoroughbred's history reveals of the almost two hundred horses imported to England from the Mediterranean Middle East only the horses from the original three bloodlines carried on the desired traits as the breed developed.

Most agree this is exactly how a breed gains respect and becomes desired by the public; it looks a certain way, performs at an expected level; and possesses the ability to consistently reproduce those traits in its offspring. While America has imported "any and all colored cobs" bred by Gypsies, the consistency in the bloodlines coming from those families identified in the early beginnings of the Gypsy Vanner Horse Society registry, as well as studies conducted by myself and others, continue to produce the horse that first caught my attention in the mid 1990's.

As I have reviewed the GVHS Studbook and visited many, many websites of individual farms representing all registries for the many Gypsy bred horses, I still am drawn back to the horses who claim a connection to those very few bloodlines. While many of those founding stallions and mares are deceased and we cannot verify parentage through DNA, we recognize we may have horses who claim heritage that is false. Given time I feel certain, if not an accurate heritage, the horse will not be able to produce what it claims it is and will eventually drop from the breeding selections of our careful breeders.

While we know that registry inaccuracies exist and may continue to show up for a few more years, the most important step is to acknowledge this truth and move forward with as accurate a record as is possible. From this point on we will know the horses. It is my belief that those who have been proven to be connected or have received word of mouth pedigrees identifying them with those early and most loved lines will as in the Thoroughbred continue to be the strong base for the Gypsy Vanner Horse breed as it grows and builds for the future.

In the meantime, I hope the GVHS will begin to applaud its founding bloodlines by educating the public as to who they are and why they are important. I also hope that truly discriminating breeders who have the dream of becoming distinguished breeders for the Gypsy Vanner Horse will choose carefully. Will begin with known pedigree to known pedigree as their basic formula which can be stated, "breed the best to the best and hope for the best". Even using this recipe, we know we cannot always get a great or even a good horse, but we certainly increase our chances.

Looking at the second circle horses (strong, correct phenotype), those in the landrace which through selective breeding continued to move further along the continuum towards genetic uniformity; making solid choices from that group to be bred back to the center circle horses (known pedigrees), those, mid '90's horses, who had become a standardized breed, is the next step in a breed building plan. This gives us horses with a broader genetic base and with the potential for strengthening the known pedigree base. Taking the resulting foals and at breeding age connecting back to a different line in the center circle continues adding to the genetic building blocks that will build the breed as a whole and in the process, produce incredibly beautiful, breed worthy representatives.

We need to help breeders move away from the current practice of breeding unknown horses to unknown horses. This is in my opinion creating a population once again of common cobs whose genetic capability becomes more and more removed from the breed expectations. We are already beginning to see the wide variance in quality resulting from these breeding choices. While there are some excellent horses with confirmed phenotype in the second circle and by breeding those horses to each other can result in yet another recognized bloodline developing over several generations, that formula can be tricky and should be done on a small scale until the resulting foals become evidence for pursuing those lines for breed building purposes.

Currently the GVHS registry contains a little over five thousand horses; a number that mirrors the total Gypsy bred horse population (both good and bad) at the time of the discovery of the selective herds. We know that in the five thousand registered Gypsy Vanners there is varied quality. While I have no doubt the registry will provide some form of education, politics will inevitably continue to play a role, therefore dedicated breeders should make an effort to become knowledgeable on what the "original intent" was with regards to quality. They should learn about, observe, and study horses from the pedigrees that have continued to produce "that quality" over time. While the Evaluation Program established by the GVHS certainly can and should be used as a breeding tool; it can only be enhanced by a population of breeders who have a clear and working knowledge of the founding pedigrees that built the breed originally. Those lines continuing to give evidence of treasured traits through twenty years of recorded outstanding progeny.

A registry is nothing more than an organized group of people who love a particular animal and seek together to recognize, preserve, and promote that animal. Such organizations are essential for maintaining genetically uniform populations for the future. Currently there are multiple registries for horses and ponies coming from Gypsies, and simply put multiple registries are not a good thing. Such an environment splits resources and preservation and promotional efforts causing confusion rather than consensus.

When you study well established breeds you find that their success lies in single registry management. Those who are in the business of researching breeds all agree that multiple registries do not serve any breed well. In fact, it is understood that breeds not only have to survive the physical environment in which they find themselves; they also have to survive political environments created by their own breeders.

Sadly, this is where we find ourselves with these incredible horses and ponies.

The two most vital functions of a successful breed registry are communication and education. Accordingly, the education program of the organization should include plans to provide information to breeders, members, and the general public. There should be guidelines for marketing that helps breeders best promote their stock through the organization's standards, goals, and programs.

Currently if you visit websites no matter the registry the owner has chosen, you will find their self-prepared promotion of their horses; their story, what they believe the breed is, or worse you find they are dual or triple registered, indicating little to no respect for what registries are designed to accomplish, very few indicate they are striving to attain or maintain the goals of a specific registry.

If a registry has 100 members this means it could have 100 versions of what the breed is unless the registry provides organizational support, guidance, and management. Currently given the political environment that exists the registries are viewed as nothing more than a means to provide papers which enable the owners to show their animals. Members for the most part are not looking to the registry for education or breeding support.

So, how do we get back on track. Some believe we have to go back to the basics. A good starting point would be:

1. If we are involved with these horses and ponies, we have to be willing to look at these horses and ponies historically.
2. We have to be willing to study the complete population of colored horses that developed between 1950 and the present.
3. We have to come to a consensus on breed definition: type, standardized, crosses, etc.

Why do I have hope that the GVHS, and by taking these steps, should become the umbrella registry?

1. In 1996 there were no registries for any of these horses and ponies.
2. The Thompsons spent four years completing a study that involved 1, 2, and 3 above.
3. Working with the original breeders they did what needed to be done to establish the world's first registry for these horses and yes, for the ponies too.

4. All other current registries formed after the GVHS and were formed for political or catch up reasons rather than for breed recognition as was the GVHS.

This is not simple; I frequently share just how complex this situation has become. Yet, I have to have faith that it is still not too late. It is my thought that if the GVHS, and I am happy to say they have as of February 2018, reinstated the three heights, since it already includes the average and taller horses which have parents in the registry; would enable the registration of the now popular ponies. By doing so the registry would then include the whole of the population which can be classified as a standardized breed.

As shared in a previous chapter, the original breed standard first written by Dennis and Cindy Thompson with the help of their Gypsy teachers, was simple and contained only seven elements along with the suggested three heights: Grand Vanner, Classic Vanner, Mini Vanner. It states the simple requirements which the Thompsons and their Gypsy teachers had agreed captured the very essence of the breed at that time. This means as of the mid '90's there were breed worthy animals that possessed all the characteristics of this new breed and they came in three heights. Cindy Thompson's dream was to see that group of animals appreciated, preserved, and promoted under the name, Gypsy Vanner Horse, and the work needed to recognize, preserve and protect such a breed conducted by the Gypsy Vanner Horse Society registry.

CHAPTER
Eleven

A Synopsis: Breed Development Research and Breed Definition

B reed recognition and the forming of registries for breed protection is always a human undertaking.

People make the choices that determine what the breed is; how it will develop; and what will the outstanding specimen ultimately look like and be able to achieve.

According to the works of breed preservationists, Dr. Phillip Sponenberg, Dr. Donald Bixby, and Dr. Deb Bennett, the following are the intricate components involved in first understanding and then maintaining a breed:

> History
> Phenotype
> Pedigree
> Performance
> Politics

Of course, the inevitability that must be understood, cautioned about, and managed is that of change. The question which must be asked is, "If we are in the business of breed preservation, then why would we choose to change it?" Yet, all breeds come face to face with the human desire for something a little different, and so it happens.

With these thoughts in mind let's take one final look at these pieces to the puzzle and make certain we comprehend each role, each contribution, and each potential impact.

HISTORY

"Understanding breed history is essential if breeders are to adequately steward the breed as a genetic resource." – (Sponenberg and Bixby 2007, 35)
This quote from the Sponenberg and Bixby work truly hits the nail on the head. In one sentence, they give us the recipe for success for any breed: understand the history behind a group of animals in order to enable a better stewardship of that group as what, why yes, a genetic resource which promises that group a future. I enjoy history. When I look at things through the lens of history I believe I can come to a much better understanding of why something is what it is; whether the topic is a government, a culture, a group of animals. Some would argue that history is written or shared by those who somehow were in charge shall we say at the time of its recording. When we research, though, the ultimate goal should always be to find as much information as possible that falls within a framework of accuracy and truth.

How we use or understand history has changed drastically in the last hundred years. In 1900 the world was a simpler place. Information came primarily through the written word; the newspaper business was booming and reporters were the source of hopefully accurate information. The printed word was protected by laws to insure its accuracy as well as to protect the reporters/writers. There was also an element of moral fiber and a respect for a system of values both of which have diminished in today's fast paced existence.

In our world in the early 1900's, history was a part of understanding; it was viewed as a starting point to research. One would be expected to seek out, learn, and improve on what had gone on before in the topic undergoing scrutiny. In today's social media frenzy, history is viewed more often than not as simply opinion, to be honest many a topic has unfortunately lost even its face value in the idea that opinion now reigns over fact.

When I first began my teaching career back in 1973, there was in every teacher's plans a seatwork page entitled, "Fact or Opinion". We taught the difference. Students were expected to know that difference and to utilize it in their understanding and responses to the world around them. An opinion was recognized by words such as: I believe, I think, I feel, etc., whereas fact was stated simply as is and was grounded in an understanding of a truth: I don't "believe, think, or feel" that *springtime grass is green*. I can see it, others before me have seen it, and it is therefore an understood reality. Therefore, to state that *springtime grass is green* is a fact, not an opinion.

In our social media age, world view has shifted. Now, through websites, Facebook, Twitter, etc. individuals are encouraged to share all sorts of information and through this barrage of instant messaging facts and opinions have blended and become to a degree one. Now when we share something we have learned much too often the response is, "well, that is your opinion." No thought is given to how or where you obtained the information; if disagreement is the receiver's attitude then your statement is reduced to opinion without further inquiry. Without a doubt this shift will in time have an impact on everything in our world to include our beloved breed of horse.

It already has.

As I have done my best to share and explain, when I first encountered these horses back in the mid 1990's in Germany, my interest was one of understanding them. Over a twenty-year period, I have acquired seven of these beauties, primarily through amazing exchanges that brought into my barn yet other examples for me to study. Finding out as much accurate information about these horses as possible was always my goal. Unfortunately, I learned very early on that the Gypsies would pose a problem by nature of who they are and how they do business; to find the Thompsons and their work was truly for me a blessing. I have tried to share why I view their work to be among the most accurate when it comes to early horses and breeders.

As time passed, more people got involved, more horses were imported, and it became imperative for me to study more. It was clear that to understand these horses one had to look at the people involved from the beginning up through the present. Why? - Because people make or break a breed.

So, what I have tried to do in this work was to follow the people and the horses. First, the Gypsies from 1900 until the present and then the Americans from 1996 through the present; after which it has become clear to me why breed preservationists include the study of historical happenings as a critical piece to understanding and then protecting specific groups of animals as breeds. History provides us with steps and/or events in the development process, the points of discovery/breed recognition, the obstacles encountered on that journey, as well as in the process of preserving the recognized breed for the future. It is here that I would like to share some of what I consider key events and players in the last two decades.

1996 – the establishment of the Gypsy Vanner Horse Society as a private registry owned and managed by Dennis and Cindy Thompson.

2002 – death of Cindy Thompson. This tragic event left the Society reeling; without Cindy's vision and energy the momentum was lost.

2002-2003 - saw the shift in leadership and other volunteers come on the scene; among those were the Kerwin sisters, Mary Beth and Kristin, who helped in so many ways. Mary Beth took on the huge task of serving as the organization's registrar. These young women traveled, documenting the horses and meeting with the owners. Today Mary Beth's website: vannercentral.com remains a valuable source of information for those wanting to know more about the Gypsy Vanner Horse.

Dennis Thompson asked Jacki Clark to serve as the Executive Director for the Gypsy Vanner Horse Society. Mrs. Clark's willingness to unselfishly provide funds for advertising and promotion at large events such as the Equine Affairs in both Massachusetts and Ohio was critical to helping the then struggling organization.

2003 – Ohio Equne Affair; prior to this event a meeting was called by Jeff Bartko and other importers of Gypsy bred horses to establish either a new registry doing away with the Gypsy Vanner Horse Society; or a registry separate from the GVHS but one that would be an official non-profit registry rather than a privately owned one as the GVHS was at the time. It would be this event that would spark the development of the multiple registries we find today. This single event stands out as an example of how politics can make breed recognition a difficult process.

2004 – Ohio Equine Affair would again be the stage for yet another historical event in the life of the Gypsy Vanner Horse Society. Jacki Clark and I were attending and representing the Gypsy Vanner Horse with Lash and my mare, Magic. Deb Putnam, Equine Affair Representative, would stop by our booth and inform us that Dennis Thompson had arrived and called a meeting of the GVHS in her office that afternoon. It is a day I will certainly never forget. There were approximately fifteen GVHS members all crowded into a less than adequate space. Dennis called the meeting to order and introduced Doug Kneis as the Society's new Vice President, and Barbara Snyder as the new treasurer. With the assistance of Mr. Kneis' attorney the required steps had been taken to make the GVHS an official non-profit registry now with these three individuals as its Founding Board.

2005-2007 – These next few years were unbridled years for the organization. I say that as they were years of political strife and decisions made during that timeframe rocked the organization and lead to some of the confusion we still are dealing with today. It would be during these years when a more lenient registering of horses would become obvious; up until this time the Thompsons had been "highly selective" in the horses they allowed into the registry and rightfully so. Now with new leadership and ideas flowing, more and more horses with unknown lineage were registered, it would also be during this time when unknown lineage of odd color became more prevalent in the registry.

2007 – This year was the year that became without question the pivot point for the Gypsy Vanner Horse Society. During this year, I would grow up, if you will, and unfortunately come face to face with the corruption so often found in the history of various breeds. I still find it difficult to recall the events of that year. The number of people involved with these horses was still small. It was a time when community had an opportunity to build, but there were those who had personal agendas and community building was the last thing on their minds. Women love horses and therefore the ones in the thick of the mix were women. Over time many of us had gotten to know each other through our involvement with the horses. As a result, friendships had formed; or I should say relationships which were assumed to be friendships had formed. A new registrar had been hired by the GVHS and she was working hard to get to know everyone. This individual controlled the records for the registry and that is a critical position. Unfortunately, she did not have the best interest of the GVHS in her plans. I would have frequent phone conversations with her and others as we worked towards building the registry, or so I thought in the early months of 2007.

As the summer slowly drew to an end, it became obvious that an unhealthy undercurrent had developed within the organization. A Board of Directors election was scheduled that autumn and given the concern I decided to run for one of the seats.

I will never forget the night I received a phone call from one of the women I considered a friend. She began to explain a conspiracy that was being set in motion by a group of women to get two ladies elected to the GVHS Board of Directors. Once elected to the Board, they along with a current sitting Director who was on their side, would form a majority and begin a re-organization of the registry, to include doing away with the name, Gypsy Vanner Horse. The person calling me was asking me to step down and not run in the election as the group felt that I would pull much needed votes away from their chosen candidates. I will never forget the feeling in the pit of my stomach when I told her that under no circumstances did I plan on withdrawing from the election. I was threatened and to this day I keep a folder housing all the emails and threats that followed. Even though I remained in the race I did not win, and their two candidates were elected.

On December 31, 2007, an emergency meeting of the GVHS Board of Directors was called. The Director who was involved with these women had been asked by the Board to step down from a position in an organization she had started which was in conflict with her position on the GVHS Board. Since she had not done so, the GVHS Board met to remove her from her Director position with the GVHS. Sadly, this individual was my friend. She had been involved with the GVHS from the very beginning and her work on behalf of the GVHS on the west coast had been ground breaking. To see her get caught up in this was heartbreaking for me and others.

However, had the GVHS Board not taken the steps they did the organization would have been threatened and who knows what it would look like today had these women been successful in their plan to overtake the registry.

2008 – In the early days of 2008 I received a call from Jerry Bratfish, the GVHS Vice President, explaining the recent events. Since my friend had been removed from her Director's seat, and since I had received the next highest number of votes in the most recent election, I was being asked to step into that seat. It was not an easy decision. However, I felt in my heart that these women I had called friends were wrong; I knew that the name, Gypsy Vanner Horse was critical to establishing these horses as a breed. It really was not about Mr. Thompson and his personality or his choices; it was about the work to recognize and build a breed. I therefore accepted the appointment to the GVHS Board of Directors.

Mr. Bratfish was happy with his one Gypsy Vanner Horse and he and his wife didn't sign up for all this drama, so shortly thereafter he withdrew from the Board. This left Dennis Thompson, Bill Ricci, and myself. Given the nature of the recent restructuring and all the internet chatter, the registry was on shaky grounds. January and February 2008 were critical decision making days. Sometimes when we reflect on such times it becomes clear just how important the people who were involved are in what would follow. There was a need for Dennis Thompson to be there, after all he and his late wife Cindy had established the registry and declared to the world that there was an unrecognized breed of horse that was worth better understanding and they had named that group of horses, Gypsy Vanner Horse. Therefore, you cannot tell the story, or there is no story, without the name, Gypsy Vanner Horse. Even if the women had been successful in their attempt to overtake the registry and had they done away with the name, Gypsy Vanner Horse as a breed name, the question would always be, well, how did these horses come into the spotlight? Ultimately they would have to tell the Thompson story and the name, Gypsy Vanner Horse would resurface.

Secondly, we needed a clear headed, respectable, intelligent, business savvy leader in the mix. That came in the person of Bill Ricci. Bill had become involved with the horses because of his wife, Wendy. She had fallen in love with the horses and in 2003 convinced Bill to buy a lovely mare with a young colt at her side. That horse would be the special mare, WR Panda Rose and the colt was the young, Tinker Toy. I would meet Bill and Wendy for the first time when they wanted to include Tinker Toy in the GVHS breed demo at Massachusetts Equine Affaire 2003. Jacki Clark and I were managing that event and Dennis introduced us to this couple and their young colt.

By 2008 Bill and Wendy had developed one of the most respected and growing breeding programs in the country for Gypsy Vanner Horses, WR Ranch. Therefore, it was obvious his interest in preserving and protecting the registry. He had a love for the breed and his business background brought logic and structure to a passionate and sometimes flamboyant, Dennis. It didn't hurt that Mr. Ricci was also a person of means. Mr. Thompson sought out such individuals and was thrilled when he could get them involved.

This three-member Board was complete with my appointment. I brought the other ingredients for success to the mix. First of all, I am a woman, and the most important reason here was balance. We all know that men and women have different approaches to problem solving so it would be extremely important to have a woman's view on the situation. Secondly, I am an educator. I know how to pull together information and present it in a concise and well organized fashion.

With these skills in our toolbox we planned the February 2008 GVHS Annual Meeting in Texas. This history is not complete without the ladies in the background. Bill and Dennis were happy for me to take on the planning of the event. I had asked if I could seek a committee to help me with the planning. Anne Crowley, Robin Visceglia, Rhonda Cofer, and Kim Osborne all provided input and support needed to make this event a positive one.

It was a time of uncertainty for the organization. People were confused. It was understood via all the information online that a large number of people were falling prey to the confusion and misinformation being generated by those wanting to do away with the GVHS and the name Gypsy Vanner Horse. Would the GVHS be able to survive in such an environment?

I am happy to share that following our 2008 Annual Meeting there was a new hope for the Gypsy Vanner Horse Society. With this shot in the arm Dennis, Bill, and I began to look at next steps. We needed a full Board for the work ahead. Rather than hold an election given the recent troubles, we decided to go with Board appointments which were allowed in our Bylaws. The search was on for the right people to complement our existing leadership. We would go through the membership list and ultimately would settle on the following: Sue Rathbone, Bob Smith, and Mike Litz. At the time, it was clear that all three realized the importance of the name, Gypsy Vanner Horse and in each of their breeding programs they sought to achieve quality.

As the work of the GVHS got underway it was evident that given the public opinion we would need to ask Mr. Thompson to step away from the Board and serve in the capacity as founder and consultant. The 2008 GVHS Board of Directors was set: Bill Ricci, Sue Rathbone, Bob Smith, Mike Litz, and myself. We began the work of rebuilding.

As history looks back on these five people and our combined efforts during this most difficult time, I believe it will see that our work laid a firm foundation on which to not only reclaim, but to build this registry and the breed.

2009 – this year set in motion yet another milestone for our registry. It was during 2009 that the Board of Directors decided to begin an Evaluation Program. An outside consultant, Wayne G. Hipsley, was hired for this most important job. While our original breed standard was simple and straight forward, most judges and equine professionals outside of our chosen breed, struggled with understanding it. Many felt its simplicity left too much room for personal interpretation. Therefore, Mr. Hipsley, who had prepared breed standards for several well know breed organizations was asked to begin this task for the GVHS. In 2009 the first seminar conducted by Mr. Hipsley was held introducing the program and the newly expanded breed standard.

This was also the first time an actual Evaluation using the program was held. The Evaluation Program has become valued and respected over the last nine years. The program's focus is of course on the breed standard and therefore the desired phenotype. While this writer certainly appreciates, and sees value in this program it is my opinion it offers but one piece of the breed development puzzle for these horses. A more complete program would also include: history, pedigree, and the effect of politics on the breed.

2013 – the next milestone for the GVHS came in 2013. This year the organization introduced and published for the first time its official publication, The Vanner Magazine. It had not been an easy task. In this fast-passed social media driven world, the idea of a paper publication seemed antiquated and obsolete. Yet, from my perspective a paper publication would offer a more stable, and accurate source of information for a general public that was beginning to be drawn to these horses and whose questions were growing exponentially. I fought the good fight and finally at the Annual Meeting in 2013 held in Las Vegas, Nevada, the General Membership voted unanimously to proceed with the first edition with me as the Founding Editor. Today The Vanner Magazine is a venue to showcase members and their beautiful Gypsy Vanner Horses; it is a much desired member benefit; and has proven to be a worthwhile component of the registry's work.

While all these things were happening within the world of the Gypsy Vanner Horse Society, the other registries were busy with their plans as well. Following 2007 the Gypsy Horse Association (GHA) formed as a rebound organization from the GVHS conspiracy movement. Its primary focus was to register horses and help get shows started. It was an all-inclusive movement. The other two registries with the strongest following in the USA were the Gypsy Cob and Drum Horse Association and the Gypsy Horse Registry of America. These two organizations have had various ups and downs over the last two decades, with the GHRA being the stronger of the two as of 2018. Again, the focus for these groups appears to be registration and shows.

With that said what had been happening in the world of these horses in the United Kingdom? As already shared with the establishment of the Gypsy Vanner Horse Society in 1996 the market for Gypsy bred colored cob type horses was suddenly open for business. I have tried to share the good and the bad of that situation. However, historically, what was the impact with regards to Gypsy breeders? The Gypsy culture was not breeding horses for the outside world, yet now the outside world was creeping into this previously somewhat guarded domain and seeking to purchase the horses. I don't believe this really changed anything for the long-time breeders; the families whose horses had already earned the respect of the culture at large. What this new American interest did do was to attract the attention of some younger, business minded, Gypsies as well as local outsiders (horse folks in Ireland and England; not Gypsy) who suddenly saw the horses from the Gypsies now in a new and more profitable light. The question, how could they get their hands on desirable stock that would attract these unknowing American buyers? They set to work buying up what they could find and busily "breeding up" herds for this purpose.

What fascinated me was how these folks suddenly had a breeding program and had a prefix they proudly put on their "new" stock. That is, they bought up what they could, mostly the hand-be-downs from the Gypsy breeders and without any thought attached these new prefixes to these horses. Suggesting to unknowing American buyers that they, these new owners, were the breeders. I can think of one team who literally flooded the market with these horses coming from all these various breeding backgrounds. It was amazing to me how gullible we Americans can be.

At the same time, many of the most respected Gypsy families had already begun back in the '90's to breed their herds down to the pony size cob, by this writing they had achieved this beautifully. Again, we have the situation where we have to ask are these ponies purebred? Well, in the most respected herds they most certainly are. How you might ask? In the 1990's these selective breeders were using their 14 hand or shorter stallions matched with their smaller purebred mares and holding back the foals that fell under 13 hands. I remember one of my favorite results was a little stallion bred by the McCann family. His name was I believe McMaster and he stood only 12.2 hands. On their overseas visit to film the Gypsies and their horses, the Barretts (Mark and Jackie) captured this lovely little one on film. It left a lasting memory in my mind. Granted there were those who chose to crossbreed with the local pony breeds to speed up this downsizing process, not unlike what we have already seen with the larger horses to obtain traits like odd color. Therefore, as people became interested in the ponies, they would have to be aware of all of these possibilities; again, the purebred groups were certainly fewer in number and that was only of importance to those who were interested in understanding any of these horses and ponies as a genetic based breed.

Registries for any of these animals were nonexistent prior to the establishment of the Gypsy Vanner Horse Society. Then overseas in 1998 the Irish Cob Society was formed, and I believe this was a catch-up effort, simply to provide a structure to accommodate the new market.

I believe in time history will both reveal and teach us that whether it was catching up by forming registry organizations or breeding up to grow herds of stock for sale, all of these were reactions, all too often done in haste to try and get in on what many realized would be the benefit of breed recognition and registry formation already accomplished by the establishment of the Gypsy Vanner Horse Society. While history will certainly contain elements of opinion, we simply must not overlook the facts that also can be found there. History is ongoing; we are building and continuing this story today.

PHENOTYPE

The logical follow-up to reviewing historical happenings within cultures and their breeding choices would lead us to the phenotype they began to like and therefore build, and improve upon over time. For the horse that would become the Gypsy Vanner Horse, there were certain ingredients which our study of history has given us that were vital parts of this recipe: size, color. They needed a smaller horse with a broken coat. History then teaches us that due to other circumstances and interests they began to choose horses with feather, more hair, and a less drafty appearance.

By the time the Thompsons had stumbled upon our beloved Cushti Bok the recipe had created the horse, thus it now had a recognizable phenotype. When Dennis and Cindy sat with Fred Walker and talked about "that perfect horse", they identified the "look" that was created when all the "right pieces" came together.

The Gypsy Vanner Horse breed standard which you can find by visiting the GVHS website at www.vanners.org is the latest version. It was written in more horse industry friendly language in 2009 in an effort to provide judges with more clarification on the traits most desired in the breed. Originally the standard had been simple including only the seven points already shared in a previous chapter and repeated here:

1. Short back in proportion to overall body (short distance between last rib to point of hip.)
2. Broad chest.
3. Heavy well-rounded hips (slab sided or severely sloping hindquarters are considered a fault.)
4. Heavy flat bone at the knee, ample hooves (small contracted hooves are considered a fault.)
5. Feathering that begins at the knees or near the hocks extending over the front of the hooves. Ample to abundant mane and tail.
6. Sweet head (fine head on a strong neck in harmony with the horse's overall look.)
7. Disposition (the horse should exhibit traits of intelligence, kindness and docility – overly aggressive behavior is considered a fault.)

In addition to these seven points the standard suggested that the breed be recognized in three height categories:

Under 14 hands – Mini Vanner
14 hands to 15.2 hands – Classic Vanner

15.2 hands and up – Grand Vanner
(Brochure: A Colorful Combination/Thompson, 2003)

It was these seven points of conformation and temperament which had provided a blueprint for the Gypsy breeders working at creating "their perfect caravan horse". The Thompsons would then record for the first time this information for the purpose of protecting this treasured phenotype for years to come.

I want to take a moment and point out if I may the age-old wisdom of too much of anything is usually not a good thing. I feel that in the beginning, and even now, many people new to horses and new to this breed got caught up in the idea that more hair was always the way to go. It is here that common sense needs to draw in the reins and recognize the need for balance. All too often people have been pulled in by all that hair and in reality, that hair has covered a multitude of conformational flaws. Feather that is too thick can cause skin problems and lead to health issues. I like the choice of words in the breed standard above: ample to abundant mane, tail, and feather. Somewhere in the middle we find excellence for the horse, for its overall health, and for us to enjoy.

The height classifications were the result of finding horses/ponies within the three height ranges. The Gypsies' selection process had started with draft crosses whose heights would have ranged from 16 hands and up; this process had reduced the height to the 14 – 15 hand horses most common in the 1990's herds. The Gypsies had already in the mid 1990's shifted their breeding choices to reduce the height even more while attempting to retain all other desired traits. When the Thompsons realized this they not only found it interesting, but considered the value of introducing a new breed that could be offered in three heights.

Unfortunately, several years ago at an Annual Meeting for the GVHS the height categories were eliminated because a GVHS member did not like the name of one of the categories. Years would go by with this being in place. I am happy to report that at the GVHS Annual Meeting in February 2018 the restrictions on the heights were lifted. The original design was now back in place.

When the breed was first introduced in 1998, these three heights were also introduced. It was the hope and intention to over time purchase and import quality horses/ponies within the three height ranges. From this writer's perspective, the following would have been stumbling blocks to finding the desired quality:

- The first and foremost problem was number of horses. The estimated total colored cob population in the mid 1990's was approximately 3000-4000. That would include all – indiscriminately bred, crosses, and selectively bred herds.
- Selectively bred herds had been estimated by the Thompsons to be about 20% of the total population. If that was the case, then you can see that the 20% would be made up of quality animals ranging in the heights found; making the number of horses/ponies in each height category significantly small in number.
- The third problem was a problem that continues to plague this breed today; the inability to educate the masses in time to make a difference.

Once the breed was introduced the public sought out the Gypsies and their horses and mass importation of colored cobs to North America got underway. The Thompsons continued their efforts but with the ever-increasing internet availability, their message was getting lost in the myriad of new websites all claiming expert Gypsy connections. While the Thompsons continued to move forward, the negotiation process with Gypsy breeders was lengthy and expensive; with Cindy Thompson's death in 2002 things came to an unexpected and devastating halt. By 2008 the registry had gone through many adjustments and in 2009 the GVHS Board opted to eliminate the height categories, due to a membership vote, and to focus on the 14 to 15 hand horse as its goal. Realizing that a height variation existed within the quality animals that had been registered the Board set the height classification in a range from 13.2 to 15.2 hands. (As indicated this was reversed 2018.)

In 2009 the GVHS hired Wayne G. Hipsley to develop from its original standard, the current Breed Standard (at the time of this writing), upon which the GVHS Evaluation Program is based. The GVHS Breed Standard and the Evaluation Program gave an organized group of breeders/enthusiasts a structure under which to safeguard phenotype. However, what must not be overlooked is that phenotype is but one piece of the puzzle to preserve a breed. The other two being history and pedigree (genetic analysis). We must not forget *"landraces and local breeds existed before the standards that describe them" – Sponenberg/Bixby 2007, 41)*

The Gypsy Vanner Horse is understood to be a portion of a landrace, resulting from isolation and selection. The Gypsy culture was a closed environment; breeding horses within that environment lead to Gypsy breeders selecting particular horses to further produce a new horse over time. The Thompsons' arrival would be viewed by breed preservationists as the founding event. To continue the horses as they were at the time of Cushti Bok's discovery all elements of this landrace would need to be understood and utilized to preserve its future: isolation of herds within the United Kingdom; selection of horses by foundation breeders identified in the Thompson study, and by others who have formed friendships with Gypsy families; the horse (phenotype and pedigree) at the time of discovery leading to breed recognition.

Phenotype is, as you can see, a critical component to first understanding and then protecting a breed for future enjoyment and use. As with any recipe, a single ingredient cannot on its own produce the desired end product. In this section on phenotype I am looking at it through the lens of breed preservation and conformation for performance. The Sponenberg and Bixby work refers to phenotype as the desired outcome of the breeding process grounded in genetics for preservation. The work of Dr. Deb Bennett, "Principles of Conformation Analysis" Volumes I, II, and III give us how conformation and therefore phenotype enable performance. We will touch on this again under the sections on Performance and Politics.

If breeders focus solely on phenotype and make breeding choices of "type to type" without seeking to know and understand the genetic backgrounds, then breed type will diminish and worse still can be lost over time. Modern type breeds such as the Pinto or Warmbloods are good examples of breeds with a primary focus on phenotype. This is done because of the need for improvement in performance or in the Pinto's case, color. Breeders in these two breeds are not so much concerned about the genetic background in their horses as they are about the resulting phenotype which then excels in the performance arena or achieves the desired color pattern. Unfortunately, as a result these horses are hindered in their ability to reproduce that much-desired end because they have limited genetic uniformity (crosses, as well as purebred stock blended) and therefore lack reproductive predictability.

Horse people, breeders, preservationists, researchers would agree that when making breeding decisions the object is to maintain or improve on the phenotype. This is done by careful selection of stallion and mare based on conformational weaknesses and strengths. For example, in the case of the Gypsy Vanner a mare with a longer than preferred back would be bred to a stallion with a short back. When we look closely at the work of Sponnenberg, Bixby, and Bennett we do find there is agreement in that the stronger mating is the one that has taken into consideration, not only the phenotypes, but the history, pedigree, and performance records of the horses involved.

According to Sponenberg and Bixby "only genetically based breeds are predictable genetic resources" and therefore are the ones which should be "targeted for wise long term management and conservation." (Sponenberg/Bixby 2007, 8) This then takes us to our next topic, that of pedigree.

PEDIGREE

We have just been discussing phenotype and its importance in distinguishing a group of animals leading to their recognition as a breed. When Dennis and Cindy Thompson saw Cushti Bok for the first time their question to the farmer was, "Is he a cross or a purebred horse?" They wanted to know if this beautiful horse was nothing more than happenstance or was there the possibility that he could be replicated. If so, they were on to something.

The next four years would teach the Thompsons that he was most certainly not a cross, but that a selective breeding process conducted by the Gypsies had led to this beautiful look. Now, the next step was to identify the animals that were consistently reproducing this look – in other words tracing the genetics behind the phenotype. As is the case with most breeds the identification of the earliest animals in the genetic chain is difficult and sometimes impossible. The best we can do is to make an effort to know as much as we can and begin to record that information.

According to Dr. Phillip Sponenberg and Dr. Donald Bixby, *"the goal of breed conservation is to include all the animals that are truly of the breed and to exclude all that are not of the breed." (Sponenberg/Bixby 2007, 20)* And this is where it can get tricky.

The Thompsons, myself, and others who have studied these horses became aware of the variety of breeding practices existing within the Gypsy community. Within this variety there was an element that seemed to extend throughout and that was color – broken coat pattern. It appeared that whether the Gypsy had bred carefully and in a selective manner or whether he had simply bred an indiscriminate animal to another, color in the form of a broken coat, was what he hoped he could retain. This resulted in a population of colored horses ranging in phenotype and ability. Therefore, the Thompsons had to first look beyond the color pattern and see what other traits in Cushti Bok made him stand out from the crowd.

Meeting the Gypsy breeders who proclaimed to have prized herds of their best horses Dennis and Cindy began to see the similarities and the connections. When I first read the Thompsons' account of their study I found myself nodding in agreement over and over again. My own experience in Germany, while certainly not as extensive as theirs, had been one of observing and studying the variety in horses coming from Gypsies. Within a relatively short period I became acutely aware of "the look" and the "traits" that were present only in that unique group of horses. Once I had this understanding I simply wanted to know how they had developed, who the horses were and who the breeders were that had been responsible for this incredible combination of traits in one horse. Some early questions were answered for me by the Thompson story, and then the last fifteen years of study added more knowledge and an even better understanding of this breed.

Cushti Bok had provided the phenotype in question. The men the Thompsons met because of him began to share the names of the horses that had left their mark resulting in herds of horses "just like Bok". In the early parts of this work on the horses and the men behind the horse I gave you names of Gypsy breeders I view as the "founding fathers". Are they the only ones? As Sponenberg and Bixby share we don't want to leave any horses out and I certainly don't intentionally wish to leave out any breeder who added to the breeding choices that gave us this horse. However, I also realize that it is simply not possible to go back in time and make certain that we have captured them all. The best we can hope for is that we have identified a core group that can show us the beginnings, to clearly recognize that our intent is to respect all that contributed; and to give credit where credit is due for the end result. What I have observed is that since about 2005 many more Gypsies have appeared, offering their information and selling their horses. Their claims almost always include that their families have been breeding or involved with these horses for decades; however, what I observe, what I see, is that their herds, for the most part, don't come close to the horses being produced at the time of discovery by the men I believe to be the original breeders of the selective herds of the 1990's.

Therefore, we must turn to the animals, where do we draw those lines separating those circles in the graph, marking the divisions on the continuum? Of course, the graph is but a representation of the development – in the earliest stages all the horses being used were crosses or indiscriminate animals. Selection began when the Gypsy community wanted their horses to be colored horses. They wanted the horses to be smaller than their earlier draft crosses and so they introduced the local ponies into the mix. There are different breeds of ponies in the United Kingdom and undoubtedly many were used.

As we look at the end result and try and backup, it appears the Dales and Fell were probably more often used in the herds that would come to be "like Bok". The Edward Hart work shares that this was the case, *"These gypsy horses started in the 1950's through crossing Dales and Fell pony mares with Clydesdale stallions, said John Shaw." – from "The Coloured Horse and Pony", by Edward Hart. (Hart 1993, 63)*

In the mid-nineties when I began my study of these horses, one could see slight variations which could be attributed to breeder selection. If the Dales pony was most often used then the resulting herd had a heftier, more cob type build, while the Fell influenced herds had a more refined appearance. Then the beauty was in trying to find and possibly identify horses from the blending of those two breeding processes. You could begin to see a new horse developing with traits and a look all its own, yet firmly grounded in its ancestral draft beginnings.

At the time of the Thompson discovery they recognized that you truly could see the breeder's mark on his horses; Walker horses stood out from Harker horses, and Harker horses were a bit different from Connors horses, or McCann horses had a tweak here and there. It was a beautiful time in the development of these horses. Today because of all the breeding choices that have been made by blending the genetics from horses in the entire landrace, we are, in many cases, losing the herds with those original unique looks.

A horse's phenotype gets our attention; the phenotype exists because of the genetics behind it. Dr. Deb Bennett makes a point of downplaying pedigree, when as suggested in the section on phenotype that it becomes the sole point of breeding decisions. She shares about breeders who go on and on about this line and that line and about breeding from that genetic base. She cautions against always breeding to what she refers to as "the famous horses". The caution is centered here on inbreeding and line breeding. These of course are important factors for breeders to take into consideration. Dr. Bennett goes on to share that a *"pedigree is not a tool for predicting the future, it is a historical document. But when the family tree of an individual is replete with well- conformed ancestors who had meaningful performance records, this represents the best expectation of genetic excellence that a breeder can obtain."(Bennett/Volume I 1998, 88)*

One of the most important things I learned from studying Dr. Bennett's work is just how important it is for breeders to develop a keen sense of observation. A good breeder has to observe not just his herd as a whole but he must look at the individual animals and their individual make-up and become fluent, if you will, in the languages of both phenotype and pedigree.

In the art of breed preservation, we walk a thin line; we have to develop a respect for foundation animals and herds that gave us the desired phenotype; once achieved we must respect the phenotype and make every effort to understand all the "right parts" that are desired. We have to make decisions about viability within the breed while making certain sufficient variability is introduced to insure the health of the breed over time. This involves respecting foundational pedigrees while welcoming horses of unknown ancestry with excellent phenotype into our breed books. This becomes a juggling act; one that must always strive for balance; once the scale tips too much in either direction we run the risk of forfeiting the original quality and beauty that drew us here in the first place.

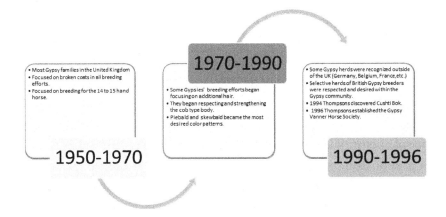

This chart gives us a visual to following the breeding choices of the Gypsy culture. One of the first things that became apparent to me in Germany when I first began my study was the variety in horses. My eye wasn't drawn to all horses coming from Gypsies; it was drawn to those that stood out, that made me want to know where they came from and who was responsible. What was their genetic map? I needed to know because I wanted to go there again and again.

It was clear to me as I observed the horses being imported into Germany the horses possessing the traits, the look, I had come to appreciate were few in number. As I have already shared the Gypsies were not telling anyone about these horses or their breeders at that time. When Dennis and Cindy did their study, and began to share their research through their website I was fascinated. Their work clearly provided evidence of my suspicions – there was a group of breeders breeding specifically for those traits and not all Gypsies or their horses were in that group.

What the Thompson research, the work of Edward Hart and others, revealed was that:

- All Gypsies had started to breed for colored horses around 1950
- By 1970 some Gypsies continued to breed indiscriminately; even though color and a smaller animal were desired outcomes even in those herds
- By 1990 a number of Gypsy breeders were more selective; began to select and hold back horses with more hair (mane, tail, feathering), a sweeter head, and most often piebald in color for their breeding programs. This process appeared to be centered primarily in the breeding programs of a few British Gypsy breeders.

In 1998 coming off a two-year study into these horses being imported into Germany and a fruitless effort to get any information from Gypsies, the Thompson research was refreshing and fueled my desire to continue to learn more.

If the Thompson work was accurate, then the horses they would import would stay true to those original desired traits; the look would be preserved through an ongoing effort to follow the genetic road map; to build the breed through continuing those lines and always returning to them for genetic strength. After all, it was this genetic base that had produced and preserved the treasured phenotype which Cushti Bok possessed when he was found. It was a respect and understanding of the "center circle – core" and reaching into that "second circle" to find the most phenotypically correct individuals and breeding them back to core animals always with complementary improvements over identified weaknesses. This kind of selection had lead, to horses like Cushti Bok, The Gypsy King, Romany Rye, The Lion King, and the score of others shared in this work that laid the foundation for the Gypsy Vanner Horse breed.

With regards to pedigree, I continue to have the utmost respect for the work that continues at Gypsy Gold farm, and at all the farms who have imported or chosen horses from those foundational genetics to build their own herds. Twenty years into the process of breed recognition, those pedigrees are remaining consistent and providing the genetic strength to further build the original intent.

PERFORMANCE

What can my horse do? The world of horses is one of competition – owners and breeders strive to attain performance recognition. Shows are developed and ribbons are won and unless those who are making efforts to maintain a breed are careful due to these undeniable influences those breeds will change. Why? People make or break breeds and most often changes are due to the need and desire to win in a performance area.

"A person might train a horse to hop like a bunny, pace like a camel or swim like a dolphin, and might then establish a breeding program that selected horses that performed best in the capacities of bunny, camel or dolphin; but he then would not be breeding horses." – Dr. Deb Bennett (Bennett/Volume I 1998, 88)

You gotta love Dr. Deb, she simply says it like it is. The truth is this happens all the time and in so many breeds – look at the Morgan, the Friesian, and the Quarter Horse. I would like to hope that we are still early enough within the development and preservation of the Gypsy Vanner Horse that we can at least put up some warning signs.

The Gypsy Vanner Horse was first envisioned by its creators as "a perfect caravan horse". What does that mean and what does a breeder have to consider in maintaining such an animal? A pulling animal has a broad chest and powerful hind quarters. If you have ever been around seasoned driving horses and their handlers you learn very quickly that a horse with a brain and a manageable, calm demeanor is required. Strength and endurance to pull weight over distance must be evidenced as this is necessary to do the job.

These were the characteristics that Gypsies not only admired in their horses, but were absolutely and without question sought out and maintained in their herds because of the performance required; they pulled the family home daily. When travel became prohibited and more along the lines of celebrations or festivals, the Gypsy culture still admired and respected the pulling horse as an integral part of their heritage and something they wanted to keep even in modern times. This desire would take us to the herds of selectively bred horses that would become the Gypsy Vanner Horse.

How extensive is the market for pulling horses? Well, if we were living in the 1800's we would be in business, but in 2018 I fear we must admit, not too much in demand. Therefore, when the Thompsons introduced the Gypsy Vanner in 1998 they of course shared its history and the Gypsy culture's intent to create "the perfect caravan horse", but at the same time suggesting the breed's performance versatility. America wants more. American horsemen and horsewomen want horses that can perform in a variety of disciplines. While a horse might excel in a particular area, it still has a greater value if it can at least compete at some level across disciplines.

The beauty of the Gypsy Vanner Horse was that it could. As more and more Americans purchased and began working with Gypsy Vanners they soon began to celebrate the breed's ability to perform in a myriad of events. As shared when I first encountered these horses, it was not as driving animals, but as calm, manageable riding mounts for beginning riding students. The horses liked to walk. They even were considered a bit lazy. It took a forceful coax to move them into their beautiful trot – which in time would be recognized as signature to the breed. I loved this about them. I felt my daughter, twelve at the time, was safe aboard this horse that seemed to think and preferred walking, over taking off at full speed at the flutter of a leaf.

Over the last twenty years more and more owners have introduced their Gypsy Vanner Horses to many performance experiences. They have found the breed as a whole is extremely willing and shows an innate interest in pleasing their humans. We have Gypsy Vanners doing all sorts of things from barrel racing, reining, sorting cattle, jumping, and dressage. At first glance as a group of breed enthusiasts we could get really excited about this. Wow, our Vanners can do anything! How exciting and wonderful is that? Well, it is exciting and wonderful within limits. However, when some owners decide to push the limits change can come about due to the horse needing a slight adjustment to its form in order to perform a particular function.

I remember back in 2003 my daughter, Jill, and I, along with Lise and Kelsey McNamara, and Dorothy Cleary had the honor of introducing the Gypsy Vanner breed for the very first time at the New Jersey State Fair. We were invited to really be the half time entertainment for their $50,000 Grand Prix Show Jumping event. Kelsey and Jill decided their mares, Fiona and Magic, could take a few cross rails and since this crowd was a show jumping one, such an effort would impress them. I will never forget the crowd's reaction when these two draft type horses seemed to fly over the rails. The picture was unforgettable; all that hair flying through the air; a solid landing and smooth recovery moving into that beautiful trot before coming to center ring for a resounding applause.

My daughter, Jill, aboard our Magic entertains the crowd at the New Jersey State Fair 2003. Photo courtesy Reflections Photography, Kingston, New York.

After our breed demonstration, we settled comfortably in our chairs adjacent the ring to watch the final classes. These beautiful jumpers were now facing five foot jumps. The jump directly in front of us was one of the most difficult and when the horses approached it they were almost standing straight up on their hind legs as they pushed off to then hopefully clear it. The athleticism was obvious in length of leg, strength of hind quarter, and an overall body type that made such a feat possible.

As I watched I thought of Fiona and Magic clearing their cross rails and knew in reality they could only compete in this event up through the two to three foot jumps. They simply would be doing harm to themselves to make attempts to take on anything more. Yet, it did cross my mind, would Vanner owners who love jumping and who love the look of the Gypsy Vanner push the envelope? Would breeders see the need to make breeding choices that would provide for a longer leg, a leaner body, to have a horse somewhat like a Gypsy Vanner; yet capable of moving further up the ladder of success in the world of show jumping?

People are already making breeding choices for taller Gypsy Vanners. Gypsies have created herds of "pony size" cobs that in my opinion look like "miniature Gypsy Vanners". Wow, Dennis Thompson was right. In a letter addressed to the GVHS Board and Officers in 2013 he wrote, *"Gypsies were breeding them down and Americans would breed them up."(Thompson 2013)* As people, breeders, and registries work with these horses, decisions will be made and the results will either respect and maintain or change the Gypsy Vanner Horse breed.

I love the Vanner as it was first uncovered, can you tell? I don't want a Gypsy Vanner that can do everything; I want a Gypsy Vanner that can do what they could do at the time of breed recognition. For me they had sufficient versatility to be an all-around horse that could be enjoyed across multiple disciplines. Would they ever be competing in the highest levels of jumping? No, but they sure are beautiful taking those cross rails, or jumping fallen logs out on trails. Would they ever compete at the top levels in dressage? No, but they certainly would wow the crowds and give owners endless hours of pleasure and success at some levels, while building incomparable partnerships.

On the other hand, if you find yourself enjoying or wanting to get involved in driving, I believe you have found the absolute perfect horse in the Gypsy Vanner. If you are a rider and simply seek a comfortable, dependable mount, then look no further than a Gypsy Vanner Horse.

I would hope that as breeders, enthusiasts and registries promote this horse, they are mindful of how their personal likes and dislikes can and will make or break this breed. I have the heartfelt hope that there will be those who see the beauty and uniqueness of the "1996 herds" and want to work together to preserve this group of animals for whole new generations to enjoy.

To paraphrase Dr. Deb, "if you breed broken coat or whatever color horses with a lot of hair that race like American Pharoah, jump like John Whitaker's Argento…., or pace like Cardigan Bay…then trust me you are not breeding Gypsy Vanner Horses."

Pictorial pedigrees as the one below will begin to assist enthusiasts and breeders in recognizing credible bloodlines, phenotypes, and performance abilities. This example is of importance to us because the breeder, Reita Parham, went further by working with trainer, Paulette Stoudt, and began to build a program where the Gypsy Vanner Horse demonstrated its performance versatility. They participated in the Gypsy Vanner Horse Society's Evaluation Program earning a truly special recognition. The stallion, "GG Oz the Wizard" and the mare, "Cushti Bok Lady" were welcomed into the Gypsy Vanner Horse Society's Hall of Fame in 2017. Oz was the second stallion, following Tumbleweed, to receive this honor while Lady was the first mare. The wonderful thing about their achievement is that to attain it their offspring must also have demonstrated not only excellence in conformation but in performance as well.

"GG OZ the Wizard", a son of The Gypsy King, "Cushti Bok Lady", the only imported daughter of Cushti Bok; and "Cushti Bok Baby", their daughter, ridden by trainer, Paulette Stoudt.

Pictured are "GG Oz the Wizard" a Gypsy King son; next is the mare "Cushti Bok Lady", the only imported daughter of Cushti Bok", shown with their daughter, "Cushti Bok Baby". "GB Cushti Bok Baby" along with her full and/or half siblings, "GB Bocelli", "GB Kapriel", "GB Shahan", "GB Sweet Lucy" made up the group of five foals whose conformation and performance scores took "GG Oz the Wizard" and "Cushti Bok Lady" to the GVHS Hall of Fame. This story is a beautiful example of what can and will happen when history, phenotype, pedigree, and performance all come together for purebred animals. It also shows how important official registries are by providing the necessary programs to clarify and showcase breed excellence.

Celebrate the Gypsy Vanner Horse and its own special set of traits that make it "the perfect caravan horse." Respect its versatility within understood limits, if you like doing something else, then maybe you need to be looking at another breed that better suits your personal performance interests. On behalf of the original founding efforts, don't change the Gypsy Vanner to suit your needs just because you can. Instead, respect it for what it brings to the horse industry.

POLITICS

"Breed survival fails when biological or political influences are mismanaged." – Sponenberg and Bixby (Sponenberg/Bixby 2007, 4)

It really all boils down to the human element, doesn't it? People first notice and desire a particular animal group for reasons of how it looks or how it performs. They embrace it; express a desire to preserve it; more often than not they change it.

"I believe protecting a breed is freezing a moment in time, not an evolution of change. The breed's purest vision is the look of a small Shire with more feather, more color, and a sweeter head; an average size horse with a draft horse body standing 14 to 15 hands." – Dennis Thompson, Co-Founder of the Gypsy Vanner Horse Society and first importer of Gypsy Vanner Horses.

In 1996 the British Gypsies responsible for selectively breeding within their colored cob herds and creating a unique group of horses which would become recognized and named as a breed, by the Thompsons, were already making breeding choices taking their herds away from the horse that had just become recognized as a breed.

Once the Thompsons imported the horses and introduced them as a rare, new breed, the door was opened for interested buyers to seek out the Gypsy breeders and also import horses. As already shared without the understanding of all the cultures involved in the development of this horse, and without the understanding of the breeding practices within the Gypsy community, horses of varying quality were imported and began to be marketed as "the same horse first introduced by the Thompsons".

Mass importation of any and all Gypsies' colored cob horses was well underway by 2003. When we look at the horses; study the Gypsy breeding practices; and recognize the development of these horses as a landrace, then we have to be conscientious about "including all that are the breed and excluding all that are not." (Sponenberg/Bixby 2007, 20)

This is not easy and becomes the responsibility of breed registries and organizations.

"Multiple breed associations serve a breed poorly." – Sponenberg and Bixby (Sponenberg/Bixby 2007, 133). Unfortunately, that is the world of these beautiful horses. In 1996 the Thompsons imported and introduced a group of horses, they had studied for years, as a new breed – the Gypsy Vanner Horse. It was their intent to educate the public not only about the horses, but the Gypsies and their history and how they had created these truly remarkable animals. The British and Irish mocked the American enthusiasm over these Gypsy bred horses; to them they were nothing but indiscriminately bred animals with little to no purpose.

The infamous Ohio meeting of 2003 revealed the battles of personalities and purposes that would splinter the already small group of Americans who had fallen in love with the horse. According to breed development research all too often we have groups involved *"who have a sincere concern for safeguarding and expanding a genetic resource to meet a particular market; while others are cynical and self-serving, and have motives that stem from a desire to cash in on the demand for rarity or to enhance their own sense of importance."*– Sponenberg and Bixby (*Sponenberg/Bixby 2007, 111*) I can honestly say that representatives from these groups were in attendance in Ohio and now years later we are not much better off.

As stated my registry of choice is the Gypsy Vanner Horse Society. I support it as the only breed registry for horses coming from Gypsies because it was founded on a study leading to the recognition of a standardized breed; the breed was then named Gypsy Vanner Horse. I, therefore, when I refer to the breed in this work am referring to the Gypsy Vanner Horse as recognized in 1996. In only twenty years the breed became recognized, named, and then politically divided. Since the founding of the Gypsy Vanner Horse Society, the Gypsy Cob and Drum Horse Association, the Gypsy Horse Registry of America, The Gypsy Horse Association, have all come into being. I invite you to look these up and read about their founding efforts and their purposes, should you so desire.

The reality is that horses meeting the specifications as Gypsy Vanner Horses can be found registered in all of these registries. Owners register their horses in multiple registries adding to the ever-growing confusion. The public is frustrated by all the names and the battles over what appears to be the same horse. Communication and education are the only tools we have to recover and take a more positive and constructive approach to preserving this breed.

"Ideally, breed associations are all involved in education. This aspect of associations is a key component to long term success of the breed and the association. All members, and especially new members ought to have reasonably detailed knowledge of the breed, its unique traits, its history, and its historic and present function." – Sponenberg and Bixby (Sponenberg/ Bixby 2007, 136)

This kind of education will build a membership body with a base knowledge enabling successful discussions and strengthening consensus for furthering the breed and organization. It is my hope that in time the community of owners/breeders/and enthusiasts will return to the founding efforts of the Gypsy Vanner Horse, come to appreciate how it came to be recognized, understand the respect owed to the founding Gypsy breeders, and honor the efforts made by the Thompsons to recognize the breed, name the breed, and establish the first registry in the world for honoring the breed – Gypsy Vanner Horse and the Gypsy Vanner Horse Society.

Once again, here are my reasons for supporting the Gypsy Vanner Horse Society as the world's single registry for these horses. In 1996 this incredibly amazing population of beautiful animals was being managed by the Gypsy culture for themselves, for their own enjoyment and benefit. They didn't care for or want any intervention from the outside world. They had already decided they wanted to breed the population down to the pony size we find today. I can speak to this personally because I observed this back in the late 1990's when I first became involved. The Thompsons discovered this on their search to understand Cushti Bok; they made a very carefully thought out decision to do the only thing that would preserve the 14 to 15 hand colored cob type horse; they decided to establish the world's first structured organization for the purpose of better understanding these animals, to declare them a breed (both type and genetic based), and to begin that work.

Their original plan was to import and register as many of that 20% as they could negotiate the purchase and to grow that group; find the "best" of the unknown pedigrees but with excellent phenotype to build on; to find the best in the different height ranges to maintain those groups effectively. With all of this work they would give credit to the Gypsy culture for this amazing accomplishment, capture their work and show the world it was breed worthy (the Irish and British communities felt that all Gypsy bred horses were mongrels), and by doing so introduce these wonderful horses to the world and give them a future. That is the historical foundation on which the Gypsy Vanner Horse Society is built. It is the only existing registry today with that history. It was not built on political dissatisfaction or strife. Its data base while it most certainly does have some questionable members, also houses the very base of that 20%. No other registry has this claim to fame. It is and was the first registry in the world for any of these horses; today we can say it is the world's first registry for this "landrace". Politics: changes in leadership, people in general have contributed both positively and negatively towards this work. Is it perfect? Absolutely not, yet I believe it is the best thing these horses have going for them and it deserves the support and involvement of all who have come to appreciate the breed.

The success of all breeds ultimately is determined by the politics of breeders and enthusiasts. With strong education and communication efforts hopefully the negative side of politics can be bridled and allow for history and science to grow the necessary base to support a future for these lovely Gypsy Vanner Horses.

CHAPTER
Twelve

In Conclusion

"Knowledge begins with experience......knowledge begins with love. Nature must be our guide...nature begins with an experience and ends with a cause.....so begin with the experience and investigate the cause." – Leonardo Da Vinci

Part I: Vanner Variations

I have to smile when I read that quote from one of my heroes, Leonardo Da Vinci. I know my involvement with these horses certainly began with an experience – seeing an incredibly beautiful horse which could not at the time be explained thus leading to my twenty plus year investigation of what it was and how it came to be. One of the beauties that the Thompsons saw in this breed was the slight variations in the selectively bred herds. They were not cookie cutter horses. With the selective herds, having been influenced by the Irish bred stallions, The Coal Horse, Sonny Mays, and others there was definitely a draft horse "thickness" to their bodies. Connors bred horses were quickly recognized by this. However, within those selective herds an "element of elegance" had begun to appear creating horses which clearly retained their draft horse heritage but had moved towards a new horse – somewhere between a draft and a regular horse. At the same time, there were without a doubt obvious similarities that put these selectively bred herds in a category all their own; an ever so slight slimming of the body; a lengthening of the neck; a head that no longer indicated draft at all; while retaining a short back, well rounded hindquarter, and wonderful bone could be seen in these new horses.

Here is yet another road if we go down it can have side trips and that is not my purpose. What I want us to do is to consider the possibilities within the breed without actually changing it. Consider divisions that broaden performance possibilities while preserving the basic phenotype and genetic base. I believe this was the hope of the Thompsons' original vision.

Let's take a moment and go back to the topic of height. The Thompsons originally established the breed with a standard that set three height categories. They saw where this would take the breed. They knew the Gypsies were already breeding for smaller pony size animals. They knew the Americans would desire taller horses. The "original 14 to 15 hand" horse had a definite place in the market already evidenced by the initial overwhelming response to the breed's introduction.

Today in England, there are fewer herds of the Traditional Cob (I use this term here for the Irish bred heavier cob type horses, i.e. The Lob Eared Horse, etc.). While the pony size cobs are becoming popular. Dennis Thompson made a plea to the GVHS Board in 2014 to reconsider opening a section for these ponies. Unfortunately, this was rejected at that time and put us years behind in getting a handle on this pony population. I believe one of the basic concerns was and continues to be how to determine herds that have recently been "bred down" by introducing Shetland or other pony breeds in the mix creating crossbred animals which would not qualify in a purebred registry. On the other hand, there is evidence of families that have successfully used the genetics from founding herds to create their pony herds by "breeding smaller cob to smaller cob" over the last twenty years and have successfully generated herds that are clearly reproducing themselves without crossbreeding with local pony breeds. Some Americans have become interested in these ponies and are attempting to establish them as a breed here.

Unfortunately, what I see is the same problem that existed with the general colored cob population in the 1990's. Not all herds had been established through careful, selective breeding, but had been the product of indiscriminate breeding resulting in obvious phenotype and quality ranges and differences. To identify the herds of truly "selectively bred ponies" would be just as great an undertaking as when the Thompsons began their work to uncover Cushti Bok's ancestors. Yet the question remains, should we go there? My thought is we must go there. This story began with the Gypsy culture making breeding choices that eventually led to a purebred group of horses, their choices over time took them to these wonderful ponies all within the same genetic base. We cannot tell the story without the ponies.

Joseph Delaney with his stallion, Galway Boy, an incredible example of the purebred pony size. The second photo is of the lovely pony size mare, Tipponi, proudly owned by Jen McNamara.

At the same time, here in America more and more breeders are seeking to create that 15 plus hand Vanner. The genetics exist within the GVHS registry given there are multiple 15 to 15.3 hand registered Gypsy Vanners to breed and either maintain or grow the height. Even Dennis Thompson began to develop a "line" of taller Gypsy Vanners and has successfully created a number of these that now other breeders have purchased to continue building this group.

"GG THE KING'S CHARMER" aka "Strider" proudly owned and loved by Crystal Lyons. Strider is a son of The Gypsy King out of the mare, Chakra. He is an incredibly beautiful example of the taller Gypsy Vanner Horse. Photo courtesy of Tracy Trevorrow Photography.

The key in going up or down has to be in maintaining, "the look" of the Gypsy Vanner Horse. Added or diminished height could shift the conformation and therefore as breeders go in either direction they must seek to maintain the desired conformation and balance of body that we expect to see in the Gypsy Vanner Horse standard. I believe just as the Thompsons originally envisioned there are a sufficient number of horses that vary in heights that will attract a following and then breeders will move in those directions. I am happy to report that in February 2018 at the GVHS Annual Meeting the height restrictions were lifted. The original intent of three heights has now been reinstated.

As previously shared in the chapter on change, another variation that has grown in interest since 2005 has been color patterns. Again, this causes us to consider whether these variations are occurring naturally within the genetic base or are we seeing crossbreeding to arrive at certain color combinations? This is another difficult question to find an absolute answer given the breeding practices of Gypsies. If we return to the original three to four thousand colored cobs at the time of the Thompson study, we know that within the selectively bred herds the preferred pattern was piebald followed closely by skewbald. Variations in color were understood within the framework of those herds. We also know that many Gypsies were continuing to breed "indiscriminately" and without question various breeds and various color patterns were found in those herds.

Are today's "odd colors" coming from those 1990's indiscriminate, less sought after herds or have Gypsies crossbred their cobs with various other color breeds to introduce these new patterns? I believe we can answer "yes" to both questions. In tracking these horses, we have to remember that once the Thompsons put the spotlight on Gypsies and their horses, suddenly given this new market all colored cobs were made readily available to interested buyers. Some of those buyers were interested in something different and with that said Gypsies set to work to offer that through color variations. Again, finding the horses whose phenotype best meets the breed standard is the best starting point for those interested in odd color horses. Then beginning to track foals and identifying quality in each year's crop will begin to move these odd colors in a safe direction to maintain the breed's correct type. Once we are a few years into such a process, we will be able to find those new colored horses who have proven that their genetics give way to quality over time. Helping breeders remember to always make breeding choices within a balance of history, phenotype, and pedigree will result in growing the breed allowing for variation but again within carefully guarded limits.

Dennis and Cindy Thompson were surrounded by all kinds of Gypsy colored cobs when they began to try and understand. They could have gotten caught up in the mystery of this unusual culture and their practices, they could have been swayed by all the stories they heard, rather they chose to seek out the heart of the breed, the truly treasured lines, the ones respected by the community as a whole. As they gazed upon these truly beautiful and remarkable herds they knew they had not only found Gypsy treasure, they had discovered the foundation of a new breed.

After twenty years of study and admiration for the lines I have shared in this work, I realize there will remain those who believe that all horses coming from Gypsies should be included in a registry, that all horses from Gypsies having found their way to America are the foundation. I have done my best to give reason based in historical information and breed development research to show otherwise. I challenge you the reader, if you are an admirer of these horses, to take a close look at the population I have outlined here, realizing that no horse is the perfect horse, and no horse will give way to excellent progeny all the time, but that the percentage of excellence and balance of history, phenotype, and pedigree should guide our choices for both breed recognition and preservation.

Part II – Hope for the Future

On my journey to understand these horses and the people behind them I came across this wonderful quote from Clifford Lee:

"We are a resourceful and resilient people who have adapted to other changes in the past thousand years. We ourselves never change. It is hard to alter a people who are content with their lot, and wish only to be what they are and always have been – Gypsies.

…..from **"Gypsies, Wanderers of the World"** by Bart McDowell (National Geographic Society; McDowell 1970, 5)

Several years ago, well known photographers, Mark and Jackie Barrett, made a trip to England and visited Appleby Fair. On this trip, they were so fortunate to interview and capture on film, renown caravan painter, Peter Ingram. When I first watched the film, I was drawn back to this interview time and time again. Mr. Ingram was sitting outside by a fire with a cast iron kettle boiling over it. You could hear the busy traffic going by and he shares how he feels so sorry for those folks hurrying off to their offices while he has the freedom to put his kettle on and ponder how to spend the lovely day before him.

Peter Ingram enjoys a pint of beer at his local pub in Selbourne Hampshire. Photo courtesy the Barrie Law Collection.

While the innovations and progress of the world around them continues, the hearts and hopes of the Gypsy remain. Their treasures are their love of an untethered lifestyle, the call of the open road, the opportunity to travel and stop at an unexpected place of beauty to spend the day or a week simply enjoying what it offers, then the choice to move on when the desire arrives.

Horses have been a part of that steadfast dream for this culture for as long as they can remember. Their love for these animals is something most of us will never understand because we don't have the connection to this appreciation of nature and its beauty. In a world where open spaces are becoming scarce, we have forgotten not only why, but how to live off and enjoy the land.

The modern, industrial, and now technological world closed in on these free spirits, but they still, even today, find time to do a "bit of travelling". The horse for many continues to be a part of their lives. The amazing "colored cob horse herds" of the 1990's continued to be adapted by their owners to the lifestyles that they were now forced to live. The smaller the horse, the more economical and easier to keep – a pony can live in a backyard space.

The Gypsy never intended or imagined his horse outside the Gypsy community. It never mattered to them if the British and Irish equestrian worlds overlooked "their treasure". While many of the young families today maintain horses, I don't believe they focus on a marketing program to sell their horses outside of the United Kingdom. In much the same way as their forefathers before they are breeding for family; they are carrying on a tradition; they have no ambitions of establishing a breed of horse. There is no structure to their breeding programs other than the "individual breeder's eye" for the "horse he likes".

To them these horses "good and not so good" are Gypsies' Coloured Cobs.

Have the herds of Gypsies' Coloured Cobs changed since the 1990's?

Yes. As Mr. Lee so appropriately put it, *"We are a resilient and resourceful people who have adapted….."* The Thompsons recognized an adaptation of the herds they had come to respect and admire in the '90's; the horses were being bred down to under 13 hands; they were becoming herds of pony size cobs. What then was happening to the 14 to 15 hand horses? They were being adapted.

Today in the United Kingdom it is not so easy to find the horse size cobs. The pony size has become the breeding focus. Is this a bad thing? No, it is this writer's intent to honor the Gypsy culture; to admire their ability to adapt to the ever-changing world around them and to maintain a connection with horses. In fact, this was the Thompsons' goal all along. This is why in their original breed standard they included three height divisions: Mini-Vanner; Classic Vanner; Grand Vanner. Through their research they could see from where the horse had come, what it was, and where the Gypsy culture was taking it.

Dennis and Cindy also could see that this amazing adaptable culture, due to who they are, would in time allow that change to erase what the Thompsons had found to be so wonderful – the 14 to 15 hand colored horse with a selectively bred genetic base that if recognized would establish it as a rare, new breed. It was this knowledge, this appreciation, which drove their decision to establish the world's first registry for the Gypsies' selectively bred herds.

Back in the 1990's as Cindy Thompson flipped through the pages of the Edward Hart book, she undoubtedly came across this wonderful quote from the Claddagh Gypsies of Galway, which would be the inspiration for their farm name, Gypsy Gold. Along with Cindy I believe many of us involved with these horses have come to truly love this saying:

"Gypsy gold does not chink and glitter. It gleams in the sun and neighs in the dark." (Hart 1993, 58)

I do see these wonderful horses as golden, as treasures. I honestly see them as so very different from all other horses; unique and rare. Maybe because I was in my forties when I was first able to own a horse and needed one that was calm and willing to work with my learning curve. This is what drew me to them. While one cannot deny the visual beauty of this breed, the real value for me has always been their intelligence and willingness; the physical beauty was just an added plus.

I see their development as surrounded by a bit of mystery and divine intervention because my look into where they came from revealed they came from a culture's love of the horse and in fact for no other reason. The Gypsy culture in its intent to remain true to heritage and tradition purposefully looked for ways to keep horses in their lives. This horse is without question a creation of the Gypsy culture, an achievement to not be overlooked or missed. One for which they deserve the credit and respect.

As I have attempted to share prior to the 1990's the Gypsy culture was going about their business, doing their thing with their horses without any disruption or recognition from the outside cultures with which they shared geography. However, once America got involved well things changed.

The initial efforts by the Thompsons clearly respected and identified the Gypsy culture as responsible for the breeding choices behind these horses. They made certain the steps taken in recognizing the horses as a breed were approved by the Gypsy men who had been their mentors on this journey. For the Thompsons, the plan was about honoring a culture through the horses it had created.

However, once the spotlight was on the horses and the American equine industry became involved things began to go awry in various ways.

1. Eager American buyers who for whatever reason set out on their own adventures to meet Gypsies and learn about the horses seemed to in many cases ignore the work already accomplished by the Thompsons.

2. Now within the Gypsy culture, the Thompson work had suggested "only a few men" were responsible for and had the "genetically strong herds"; yet, suddenly any and all Gypsy men with horses claimed they could and would offer "their colored cobs" for sale to these Americans.

These two facts alone contributed to mass importation of any and all colored cob type horses to America by those wanting to get in on the rarity and make money while it lasted. Time had not allowed for a better understanding of the population as a landrace with wide variety.

Some of these Americans began quickly to work towards breeding programs that would make a name for themselves. These folks eliminated the "Thompson story" from any of their promotions; somehow telling "their story" as a starting point for quality they proclaimed could be found "primarily in their herd alone". These Americans with fame on their mind, briefly thanked the Gypsy but wanted to claim the real accomplishment with these horses belonged to their insight and breeding choices, not the Gypsies.

With that shared did Americans steal Gypsy treasure? I have to conclude that some of them certainly tried. In the recent years, there has been a movement both by buyers here in America as well as overseas to make a turn around and give credit solely to the Gypsies once again;

even to the extent of recapturing the older terms used as names like Gypsy Cob, Gypsy Colored Cob, Gypsy Horse, etc.

Observing these events leads me to compare our wonderful "Gypsy treasure" to the actual element, gold – how it is discovered, mined, refined and used to make beautiful things admired by many throughout the world. Without the mines first being discovered none of the other things could happen. While the Gypsy people certainly loved their horses, saw and understood their value, if kept within the cultural community alone few outsiders would have ever had the opportunity to appreciate this remarkable accomplishment. It was when Dennis and Cindy Thompson chose to actively pursue and understand a little stallion that a door was opened for the rest of us to look inside. Once the Thompsons introduced their findings, the reaction was not unlike the gold rushes of old, many running to see if they too could uncover their own mine. However, as with real gold searches, some sadly got taken in by "fool's gold".

As with the element gold, there is a process, such has to be the case for these horses if we want to recognize, understand, and preserve the quality that lead the Thompsons to use that old saying from the Gypsies and refer to the horses as "gold". If we follow that process we recognize that the earlier terms being used to identify the horses left much to be desired and that by researching and understanding the quality and where it came from the work of the Thompsons lead them to know a "name" was needed as a marker for that quality, thus the name, Gypsy Vanner Horse.

The rest is history and I have done my best to take you on that historical journey from the early 1990's to today. The Gypsies' gold has been mined; some breeders have remained true to old lines and made strong breeding choices to preserve those, while others have experimented with a variety of mixed genetics creating in some cases beautiful new lines, or sadly in some diluting the original. Politics has done its worst, making too many believe the horses are all the same, leaving the community both here in the USA and abroad reeling – creating an environment beleaguered with distrust and personal gain. Currently our future path appears uncertain, I can only hope that all the good in this takes all of us and these wonderful horses to a future where respect is found for the Gypsy men whose original choices gave us something we could without doubt call "treasure". I also hope that future gives respect to Dennis and Cindy Thompson for their efforts in recognizing what the Gypsy culture at the time claimed was "their best".

I have a dream that one day there will be only one registry for these horses and ponies. I hope that registry will be the Gypsy Vanner Horse Society and the name Gypsy Vanner Horse will remain a brand marker for quality and the highest standards for the breed that had its beginnings in the meadows and glens of the United Kingdom and found its name in America. I hope that registry will respect the founding Gypsy families, honor the founding work of the Thompsons, build the breed respecting the desire of individual breeders to attain color and height variations always guided by core genetics and the Gypsy Vanner Horse standard; and that education will begin to lead breed preservation efforts making way for an even greater and exciting market. As I close this work I have an excitement that this wonderful horse and pony is growing in popularity; that equine enthusiasts around the world are beginning to see its potential; and with each new foal I celebrate the legacy and have hope for the future.

Babes, a Robert Watson bred stallion who
is pure gold.
(Photo courtesy Mark J. Barrett)

A HIDDEN TREASURE

By Joyce M. Christian

The sun shone bright on the road ahead,
The day so young and full of hope…
Gave rise to dreams and adventure's thread,
As the wagon creaked down the winding slope.

The piebald pulled with effortless might,
A family, their home, and all they owned.
From daybreak until the star-studded night,
The horse did his job; his skills were honed.

Unlike other horses he so often passed,
His ears bent forward by children's laughter,
This horse was special and even quite blessed.
He loved their giggles, as they lead him to pasture.

Picking up the reins his master's eyes sparkled true,
A pride and love felt in his touch.
This piebald had blood that was blue,
While coins of silver, the Gypsy had not much.

Passing through villages, the family's secret was safe,
The beautiful piebald plodded on until night.
Many people they passed throughout that day,
None guessing that gold was now black and white.

REFERENCES

Bennett. 1988. *Principles of Conformation Analysis Volumes I, II, and III.* Maryland: Fleet Street Publishing Corporation.

Evans. 1999. *Stopping Places.* Great Britain: University of Hertfordshire Press.

Hancock. 2002. *We Are the Romani People.* Great Britain: University of Hertfordshire Press

Hancock, Kyuchukov. 2005. *A History of the Romani People.* Pennsylvania: Boyds Mills Press.

Hart. 1993. *The Coloured Horse and Pony.* Great Britain: J.A. Allen & Company.

Law. 2000. *Gypsy Memories: A Third Selection of Photographs.* Huntingdon, York: Peter Turpin Associates.

McDowell. 1970. *Gypsies: Wanderers of the World.* The National Geographic Society.

Morris/Clements. 1999. *Gaining Ground: Law Reform for Gypsies and Travellers.* Great Britain: University of Hertfordshire Press

Sponenberg/Bixby. 2007. *Managing Breeds For A Secure Future: Strategies For Breeders And Breed Associations.* North Carolina: The American Livestock Breeds Conservancy.

Thompson. 2003. *Brochure: A Colorful Combination.*

ACKNOWLEDGEMENTS

I want to especially thank Dr. Ian Hancock for opening his personal archives at the University of Texas at Austin for me. It was there on so many pages of wonderful works that I encountered the amazing rich history of the Gypsy culture. This history has helped grow my understanding of the horses, and my appreciation for the people who developed the herds that would become a breed.

I want to say thank you to Dr. Phillip Sponenberg for being willing to work on a special GVHS project with me several years ago. While clearly the timing was off and the GVHS was not ready for what this work could have provided, it gave me the opportunity to have conversations with you, someone I hold in the highest regards when it comes to breed development research. You answered so many questions, and provided insight which encouraged me to write this book.

I want to say a truly special thank you to Dennis Thompson. Your wonderful stories, your ongoing dedication to the Gypsy people and the horse they shared with you and Cindy, continue to inspire and encourage all who find this breed. Your breeding program at Gypsy Gold set the bar high for breeders who would follow and continues to build a dream you began twenty plus years ago.

I want to say a special thank you to Mark and Jackie Barrett for always supporting whatever work I set out to do with your incredible photography. Your work has helped to introduce so many people to our beloved breed in such a magical and amazingly beautiful way.

Printed in the United States
By Bookmasters